Jeff,

All the

Ken

D1544488

Project Management
Accounting

Project Management Accounting

Budgeting, Tracking, and Reporting Costs and Profitability

Second Edition

Kevin R. Callahan (signature)

KEVIN R. CALLAHAN
GARY S. STETZ
LYNNE M. BROOKS

WILEY

John Wiley & Sons, Inc.

Published by John Wiley & Sons, Inc., Hoboken, New Jersey.

Published simultaneously in Canada.

For general information on our other products and services or for technical support, please contact our Customer Care Department within the United States at (800) 762–2974, outside the United States at (317) 572–3993 or fax (317) 572–4002.

Wiley also publishes its books in a variety of electronic formats. Some content that appears in print may not be available in electronic books. For more information about Wiley products, visit our web site at www.wiley.com.

Library of Congress Cataloging-in-Publication Data:

Callahan, Kevin R.
   Project management accounting: budgeting, tracking, and reporting costs and profitability/Kevin Callahan, Gary Stetz, Lynne Brooks.—2nd ed.
     p. cm.
   Includes index.
   ISBN 978–0–470–95234–4 (hardback); ISBN 978–1–118–07821–1 (ebk);
ISBN 978–1–118–07822–8 (ebk); ISBN 978–1–118–07820–4 (ebk)
   1.   Project management—Accounting.   2.   Cost accounting.   I. Stetz, Gary S., 1962-
II. Brooks, Lynne M.   III. Title.
   HD69.P75C354 2011
   657'.42—dc22

                                                                              2011002028

Printed in the United States of America

10 9 8 7 6 5 4 3 2 1

To my wife, Angela, and my son, Gary

To Jim, for planting the first seed

To Tracy and Susan, for their love
and generosity of spirit

Contents

Preface

Over the last few decades project management has moved from its roots in industries such as construction and defense into the mainstream of American business. Many different industries, in particular the service sector, rely heavily on Project Management as an integral part of a successful strategy. In support of the widening importance of project management, a number of important professional organizations, such as the Project Management Institute, have been created and are thriving in the twenty-first century.

As project management has been recognized as a valid career path that many have chosen to pursue, many training programs have been developed, and it is now possible to pursue both undergraduate and graduate degrees in project management. Project managers who practice the profession today come from a myriad of backgrounds, most often having started as specialists in an area of expertise and gradually moving into project management. And there lies the rub!

In our previous book, *The Essentials of Strategic Project Management*, we established the primary link between a company's mission, objectives, and operations. Senior project managers who wish to remain at the top of their profession need to understand not only the methodology, tools, and techniques of the profession in order to be successful, but they must also understand the business context within which they work. Many, if not most, project managers come from areas of expertise outside of business, and most do not have the formal education in business, accounting, or finance required to take their skills to the higher level.

Project management accounting is much more than considering how project income and expense impact the general ledger. The topic encompasses traditional accounting, cost accounting, budgeting, financing, cash flow, and earned value along with the more quantitative subjects. Project management accounting also includes such areas as strategy and executive decision making, portfolio management, and the more traditional phases of project management.

Project Management Accounting: Budgeting, Tracking, and Reporting Costs and Profitability is meant to improve the business skills of project managers. The volume contains the basics of project management accounting and finance, including insights into cost accounting, budgeting, and tracking project profitability. Most important, it provides project managers with a foundation of knowledge about the basics of business practices necessary to apply new skills to projects that they manage.

Chapter 1 is an overview of Project Management as it relates to a company's Mission, Objectives, and Strategy. Chapter 1 also points the reader toward particular topics of accounting and finance as they relate to project management. Chapters 2 and 3 are two parts of an introduction to the business basics; the former contains important foundational knowledge and the latter a case study that illustrates how to analyze a company's financial information in order to choose the right project and understand how to apply proper accounting principals to a project. Chapters 4 through 6 contain fundamental information on different areas of accounting and financial expertise, such as cost accounting and budgeting. Chapter 7 contains a comprehensive case study that illustrates how to develop a project budget based on a company's financial performance and needs. The case study integrates the knowledge, skills, and techniques of the previous chapters.

The second edition *of Project Management Accounting: Budgeting, Tracking and Reporting Costs and Profitability* includes a new chapter that will increase a project manager's skills in the area of risk management. The new chapter expands a project manager's knowledge base by introducing risk assessment from an accounting and auditing point of view. Chapter 8 will introduce project managers to a different professional approach, enhancing their knowledge of the business environment.

We hope that you will find this book useful in your quest to become a top-performing project management professional.

KEVIN CALLAHAN
GARY STETZ
LYNNE BROOKS

Acknowledgments

There are always people to thank when you have taken up an endeavor such as authoring a book. In particular, we would like to thank the Faculty and Staff of the Executive MBA program at Mendoza College of Business at the University of Notre Dame. There are many individuals there who make that a great program, but in particular we would like to thank Professors Ken Milani and John Affleck-Graves, who laid the foundation on which this effort was built.

We would like to thank Vince Malina, George Beardsley, and Catherine Callahan for proofreading and correcting our manuscript.

We would also like to correct an error from our previous book, *The Essentials of Strategic Project Management*. During the production of that book, we had an excellent intern, Erin Ellis. Unfortunately, Erin was not properly identified, and we wish to correct that here and thank her for the hard work and professionalism that she applied to the project.

K. C.

G. S.

L. B.

CHAPTER 1

Project Management and Accounting

In today's business world, we often hear the terms "strategic alignment" and "mission and objectives." Usually these terms are used in phrases such as: "We must ensure that our business units are strategically aligned with our mission and objectives." In many companies, large and small, it often seems that one area of a company does not know what is happening in other areas; in some cases, one area may even be working against other areas within the same company. Quite often there is a large gap between what the top levels of the organization are saying and what is happening at an operations level within the company.

In our last book, *The Essentials of Strategic Project Management*, we spoke about the STO model.[1] STO stands for strategic, tactical, and operational. These three levels of operation inherently have typical communication problems that many companies need to deal with (see Exhibit 1.1). Each level of the model represents a different level of a company. Strategic is the executive level, where decisions are made about the purpose and direction of the organization. Tactical is the management level of a company, where decisions are made as to how to carry out strategy. Operational is the lowest level of the company, and represents where people actually execute the work.

EXHIBIT 1.1 Strategic, Tactical, and Operational Model

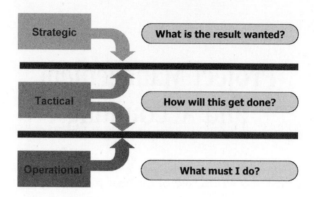

Mission, Objectives, Strategy

In order to have a clearer understanding of what Mission, Objectives, and Strategy mean, we need to look at some definitions and examples. Mission, first of all, is a statement of the purpose for the company's existence. An example of a simple mission statement could be General Electric's: "We bring good things to life." It is simple and easy to understand. Honeywell's mission statement is quite eloquent in its simplicity: "We are building a world that's safer and more secure, more comfortable and energy efficient, more innovative and productive."

In each case, the company's reason for existence is stated clearly and simply, giving direction to all that the company does. The reality is, however, that carrying out that mission is usually much more complex than a simple statement. Problems arise when management is not able to turn a mission statement into action and employees do not understand how their work carries that statement forward. That situation is where mission is often confused with strategy.

Strategy consists of a series of concrete actions that a company performs in order to carry out the mission. Each concrete action is an Objective. The actions must support the mission of the company but must also adhere to good business principles. One of the fundamental responsibilities of a company is to create a return for its owners, whether they are a small group of investors or a large group of stockholders. There is always the responsibility to do this in an ethical manner, so that carrying out the mission and creating value are dual fundamental principles of any business. Even a not-for-profit company must create value; without the money, there is no mission.

An example of a Strategy that might correspond to Honeywell's Mission Statement might be to create a new line of home heating furnaces that are highly efficient and cut down on the amount of heating oil that is used to maintain the home's temperature. An Objective for that Strategy would be to carry out research into new technology for heating oil burners that are more efficient.

Problems arise in many companies when the mission is not understood at all levels, which brings us back to the STO model. When communication does not exist between the different levels of a company, mission cannot be translated into strategy and cannot be carried out by employees. Often the walls between levels exist, as illustrated in the STO model, not because of purposeful action or a desire to harm the company, but simply because no one at the firm has tried to bridge the gap or because someone has tried and failed.

As mentioned in the preface, senior project managers have their roots in many different areas of expertise, but the great majority do not come out of finance or accounting. At the same time, in order to advance within an organization, project managers need to acquire knowledge beyond their areas of expertise. The first step toward advancement is to become proficient in project management knowledge and skills in order to have the flexibility to move beyond those areas of expertise.

After becoming a proficient project manager, continued experience in project management helps project managers attain senior status. After years of managing larger and more complex projects, senior project managers often aspire to making greater contributions to their organizations. One way to do this is by gaining expertise in finance and accounting, thereby enabling them to view the organization from a different perspective and to make a greater contribution to it.

In this chapter, we review the project management phases from the perspectives of various project management deliverables and processes with an eye to related finance and accounting issues. This review serves as an introduction to how finance and accounting is related to project management and can serve to help an organization perform projects in a manner that supports sound financial and accounting management. As we review each project management phase, we discuss the questions for finance and accounting implied in that phase and indicate which chapter in this book contains pertinent information.

Information Collection

Information collection is a crucial element in project management, finance, and accounting. Collecting the correct information is crucial for project success. We conduct our review of the project management phases according to the project management documents that are created during each phase of a project:

- Initiation: Project charter
- Planning: Work breakdown structure, project schedule, project budget and cash flow, resource plan, procurement plan, quality plan, risk response plan

  If the project is for an external client, there may be a request for proposal and corresponding proposal and a contract or some other agreement for services.
- Project Execution and Control: Status reports and dashboards.

In the remainder of this section, we look to each of these documents for information that is important to understanding the financial health of the project.

Project Initiation

The project charter contains high-level information about the project, including deliverables, stakeholders, and, in particular, the definition of success for the project. That definition ought to include a description of the financial success of the project and how it will be measured. This definition provides the guidelines by which project performance may be judged.

During initiation, the first questions concerning finance and accounting are broached. For example, does the project align with the organization's strategy, in particular the financial strategy? Does the project deliver a product or service that is compatible with the goals and objectives of the organization? Will the project create value that is within the required return that the organization's financial strategy and owners or shareholders require? Often project sponsors ask what a project's return on investment (ROI) will be. In fact, project managers can increase their contribution to the organization not only by understanding a project's ROI but also by understanding in detail how that return will be delivered, over what period of time, and at what cost to the organization.

For example, let's say that a project will have a 10 percent ROI. However, if that return is over a 10-year span at 1 percent annually, it probably would not be considered as valuable as a project that will return 10 percent annually for 10 years. But even a 10 percent return over 10 years would not be very interesting if the organization's cost of capital is 15 percent. In addition, if the project is considered very risky, then the organization may require a 20 percent annual return.

Financial levers—ways in which the finances of a company can be adjusted—are explained in Chapter 2. There are additional illustrations in Chapter 3. The case study in Chapter 7 gives specific examples of how portfolio management can require criteria based on the financial strategy of the organization.

Project Planning

Work Breakdown Structure and Project Schedule

The Work Breakdown Structure (WBS) contains a description of each deliverable that makes up the final project deliverable along with the tasks that must be performed in order to create each deliverable. Each task also has a description that defines the inputs, outputs, materials, and resources required to complete the task. The task description also defines how long each resource must work to complete the task as well as how much of each material is required.

The project schedule arranges each task in its proper order of execution and indicates the order in which the tasks must be done. The project schedule also defines task dependencies, that is, which tasks must be completed before other tasks may begin. Based on these calculations, project managers know when tasks must be carried out and what the end date for the project is, as well as what its critical path will be.

Understanding how much work must be performed is crucial to creating the project budget. During execution, one of the elements of project control is collecting information about how each task is executed. If managers do not have an accurate measurement of the expenditure of resources and materials, then they cannot determine the actual cost of a project or understand how the project is performing financially.

From the task description, project managers know the amount of effort that is required to complete the task. They also know when the task is supposed to be completed. Two basic questions yield information that is needed to get to the true state of the project:

1. How many hours (or days, if the effort is described in those terms) have the resources been working on the task?
2. How many hours (days) remain to complete the task?

The answers to these questions yield valuable information. By totaling the two answers, it is easy to find out if the task is taking more effort than expected and to come up with a prognosis on whether the task will be completed on time. Multiplying both the number of hours worked and the hours remaining to be worked by the hourly rate for each resource reveals not only the cost of the resources to that task, but also how much additional cost will be needed to complete the task. Later in this chapter we cover the concept of earned value, which explains how to work with and interpret this information.

Another concern that project managers monitor by reviewing effort on tasks and the state of deliverables is "gold plating." Gold plating is adding more to a deliverable than is required by the project specification. It is often a problem on client projects, where resources, with good intentions, seek to add value by doing more than required. It is also a major source of effort overruns on many projects. The problem also may be scope creep, where a project stakeholder has requested that additions be made without getting proper authorization.

Project Cost

Chapter 4 covers the notion of cost as it affects a project. It is important to understand the difference between cost and expense. The notion of cost deals with what must be given in exchange for the value that the project creates. For example, the hourly rate or salary of resources employed is a cost to the project. The way that resource cost accumulates will have an effect on the value created. For example, a contractor charging an hourly rate to a project will affect cost differently than a salaried employee.

7

Expense deals with the accumulation of charges that make up the project budget. In addition to salaries and hourly payments to resources, materials, overhead utilities, and other resources may make up the budget. Chapter 7 covers how to develop and monitor the project budget as well as how to develop and monitor a project cash flow diagram. The cash flow diagram illustrates the timing of cash outflows and inflows as described in the project budget.

Resource and Procurement

The resource plan and procurement plan contain estimates on resources, including the skill sets needed, as well as a list of the actual resources and materials needed to complete the project. The resource plan also describes which internal resources are available and what resources will be needed from outside the organization. It also contains information about the source of resources and an estimate of the cost. This information is important in developing the project budget.

The procurement plan is very similar to the resource plan, except that it covers other materials that are needed for the project, along with estimated costs. The procurement plan addresses timing and delivery and indicates whether there are any special situations, such as volume discounts. In a manufacturing or construction environment, the procurement plan is of great importance; it is much less important in some service industries.

During project execution, project managers must monitor the actual use of resources against the resource plan. Resources reporting on actual time spent on project tasks and estimates for task completion provide the basic information of resource cost. However, project managers must also compare the actual results against the resource plan to ensure that the resources being used match what is in the plan.

For example, a shortage of internal resources could necessitate the use of external resources that are more expensive and add to project costs. Variances in actual project performance, including scope changes, could also have an effect on resource cost; for example, tasks may have been underestimated or for some other reason may be taking longer to complete or requiring more resources. Additional resource needs can also be a problem that is not related to finances. Increased overtime for salaried employees can have an effect on other work within the organization or on general morale. Close monitoring of the resource plan against actual results helps project managers maintain the financial health of the project.

Project managers also monitor the project procurement plan, both for cost to the project and for any changes in the business environment that could affect the availability or cost of any materials required for the project. As this chapter is being written, the cost of gasoline and other fuels has become quite volatile, which would have a negative effect on any project requiring the use of heavy machinery or other equipment. If no pricing guarantees are negotiated ahead of time, or if quantities needed are greater than first estimated, there could be significant cost overruns on the project, threatening its profitability.

Chapter 4 covers information about cost, and Chapter 7 illustrates the effects of resources and procurement on project finance and accounting.

Quality

The quality plan needs to be considered in conjunction with the WBS. Asking questions about the intended deliverable in comparison with what the tasks are actually delivering provides additional information about how the project is progressing. Project Managers need to ask, "What is the deliverable and what does it do (or what is it intended for)?" The answers to these questions are the start of quality management.

In Chapter 4, we discuss the cost of quality, including prevention, correction, and warranty. During project execution and control, project managers monitor the cost of quality by ensuring that any work related to quality prevention is completed and by determining whether any correction work is necessary.

If preventive work is not performed, the overall cost of a deliverable may be lowered; if that results in increased correction costs, the project may fall short of financial goals. Project managers must monitor whether prevention costs are in line with budget, and if not, why. The need for more corrective work than anticipated could have a negative impact on project financials immediately or in the future, if warranty costs (the most expensive) are incurred.

Risk

There are several ways to look at risk. From a project management point of view, risk is quantified and dealt with through a risk response plan, seen below. From an accounting or audit view, Chapter 8 presents a comprehensive overview of dealing with risk. The risk response plan answers these questions:

- What risks threaten the project?
- What is the likelihood that a risk will occur?
- If the risk occurs, how serious will it be?
- What can be done to mitigate the occurrence of the risk?
- What is the plan if the risk does occur? What is the backup plan?

Many methods are used to calculate the effect of project risk, some quite sophisticated in their analysis and requiring detailed information. Whatever method is used, the outcome is usually quantified as a project cost. In other words, what will it cost to mitigate for risk, and what are the potential costs if risk occurs? The potential costs are often expressed as contingencies and the amount of resource time or money that is budgeted for use if risk occurs.

Project managers monitor risk in much the same way that they monitor quality. They must ensure that mitigation activities occur as planned, and thus increase cost. Project managers must also monitor for signs that risk may happen, in order to be ready to implement the risk-response plan. A timely response to risk and the judicious use of contingency often can make or break a project financially. Chapter 7 contains pertinent information for risk management as part of budget development. Chapter 8 takes on Risk Assessment from a different point of view, that of an accounting professional, providing an additional body of information to the project manager.

Project Execution and Control

A Guide to the Project Management Body of Knowledge[2] defines project execution as coordinating people and other resources to carry out the (project) plan. This definition is deceptively simple; under the direction of the project manager, the project team, vendors, and others carry out the tasks that are defined in the project plan in order to produce the project deliverables.

However, project managers must not only ensure that work is progressing as planned, but also must monitor all aspects of project execution, in particular the financial results. This is project control, which ensures that project objectives are met by monitoring and measuring progress regularly to identify variances so that corrective actions may be taken.

Project Management is not unlike flying an airplane. Flying conditions are perfect as the plane heads toward its destination. However, even on a clear day, wind currents in the air can push the airplane off course. As the pilot monitors the gauges, she will notice if this is occurring and will compensate by steering the plane back in the other direction, toward the intended destination.

The project manager is the pilot, always monitoring the gauges and ready to steer the project back on course. There is more to flying the airplane than just steering it. The pilot is always monitoring the systems, making sure that there is enough fuel to reach the destination and that all of the systems are functioning properly. If the plane runs short of fuel or if a system malfunctions, the pilot can decide what to do next to correct the problem.

So, too, the project manager is at the controls, monitoring the project to ensure that value is actually created for the organization. A number of the gauges or controls that the project manager monitors may be financial controls or quality controls. A project may be on time and deliver what is intended, but if there are cost overruns, for example, the project may not deliver value to the organization. Even an on-time, on-budget project may suffer from quality defects, costing the firm money and reputation later on.

Communication

Communication planning is the process required to ensure timely and appropriate generation, collection, dissemination, storage, and ultimate disposition of project information. Information distribution during project plan execution is the execution of the project communications plan. Carrying out the communications plan is a crucial factor in project success, especially when it—the plan—pertains to the project sponsor and other high-level stakeholders.

Communication is the real glue that holds the STO model together. During project execution, two-way communication through all levels of the organization is vital. If project initiation and planning have been done properly, then the project will be in alignment with the firm's mission and goals. The project charter will communicate organizational strategy to the project team and other stakeholders. There also must be appropriate communication back to the strategic level in order to ensure that the executives of the organization are aware of what is happening.

We talk about the appropriate level of detail in the next section, but we would like to point out a serious error that frequently occurs during projects. Often, when there are problems occurring in a project, the problems are not known, either due to a lack of project control or because the project team does not want to reveal them. It is vitally important that the project manager control the project closely and report on any problems as soon as they are discovered.

Project Control

Project control consists of one primary process: project status reporting. There are four secondary processes: schedule control, change control, risk control, and quality assurance control. These sub-processes all depend heavily on information collection and information distribution.

SCHEDULE CONTROL   Schedule control consists of monitoring the project schedule to determine if the project is on schedule and making any necessary changes. The most important tool used in schedule control is earned value estimation.

EARNED VALUE   Earned value calculations express the amount of value that a project has created at any given point in the project in relationship with the amount of value that should have been created at that point. Earned value can be expressed in terms of schedule or cost. Earned value management is a technique used to integrate a project's scope, schedule, and resources and to measure and report project performance from initiation to closeout. It is a technique that is rarely done manually, but it is helpful to learn how earned value is calculated in order to understand the premise behind the calculations and the results of earned value. We spend some time explaining earned value here, and then apply the concepts in conjunction with finance and accounting principles in Chapter 7.

   To illustrate how earned value is calculated, let's take an example. Suppose that we have a task that is scheduled to be done by one person and will take 50 hours over the course of two weeks (Effort = 50 hours, Duration = 2 weeks). The effort will be evenly divided between the 2 weeks, 25 hours each. So the planned value equals 25.

EXHIBIT 1.2 Calculating Schedule Performance Index (SPI)

Time Estimated to Complete Project = 50 Hours

Duration of Project = 2 Weeks

Planned Value = 25 (25 Hours per week)

Results:

Actual Time Needed in First Week: 30 Hours

Additional Time Required: 40 Hours

Actual Percentage of Time Completed on Project: 43% (30/70)

Earned Value = Actual Percentage × Total Time Required (43% × 70) = 21

Schedule Variance = Earned Value – Planned Value (21−25) = −4

$$\text{Schedule Performance Index (SPI)} = \frac{\text{Earned Value}}{\text{Planned Value}} = \frac{21}{25} = 84\%$$

At the end of the first week, the person performing the task reports that she actually worked on the task for 30 hours. She also reports that she will need an additional 40 hours to complete the task. This means that, in addition to some poor estimating, she has actually only completed about 43 percent of the work, or what should have taken roughly 21 hours, so the earned value is 21. Exhibit 1.2 shows the calculations that we would apply.

The Schedule Variance is a negative number, indicating that the project is behind schedule. The Schedule Performance Index (SPI) of 84 percent tells us that for every hour worked, we are getting only 50 minutes' worth of value created (60 minutes times 84 percent equals 50 minutes).

These numbers actually tell us more. When a project does not use earned value and simply relies on completion date of tasks to calculate progress, a problem could arise. Suppose that the resource in this anecdote actually finished the task during week 2, and it did take an additional 20 hours. If only completion was tracked, it would seem that all is well. However, completion alone does not tell us what effect this problem had on other tasks. In total, the resource worked on the task for 20 hours more than planned. We must ask why this happened. Is it an isolated incident, or is it a sign of other schedule problems? What other tasks suffered because this one took longer to complete and cost more than estimated?

The calculations in Exhibit 1.2 tell us that the task is over cost. The cost performance index also tells us that for every dollar spent, only $.70 worth of value is being created. We can ask the same questions that we asked about running behind schedule. While this is only one task over cost here, again, even if a small percentage of other tasks are also over cost, the financial effect on the project could be significant. To see how significant, we can apply the formula for estimate at completion, which calculates the end cost of the project based on the present results.

What we can see from the last set of figures in Exhibit 1.3 is that this project will run over cost by more than $170,000, a serious cost overrun. Yet if we do not calculate earned value and only track when tasks are completed, we risk not being aware of problems until much too late in the project, perhaps even just at completion.

Many organizations do not calculate earned value for their projects. One of the main reasons is that they don't plan projects; it is very hard to track something that is not planned. Some organizations do plan, but do not collect the information necessary to do the calculations. Tracking resource hours and other expenses against the project schedule and calculating earned value will not guarantee that projects will always be on time and on budget, but it will guarantee that if there are problems, project managers will be alerted much earlier and have a better chance of correcting the problems.

EXHIBIT 1.3 Estimate at Completion

Budget at Completion: $400,000

Cost Performance Index: 70%

$$\text{Estimate at Completion} = \frac{\text{BAC}}{\text{CPI}} = \frac{\$400,000}{.70} = \$570,000 \text{ (approximately)}$$

Consider this example: A task is supposed to take one person 30 hours to complete over two weeks, about 15 hours each week. At the end of the first week the resource has spent 22 hours and has about 18 hours left to work on the task. We now know that the task will take a total of 40 hours to complete, which is 33 percent more time than allotted for in the task description. Although the task may be completed at the end of the second week (on time), we already know that if it takes the time predicted, the task would be 33 percent over budget.

We must also consider that if work originally scheduled to take 15 hours actually took 22 hours, how do we know that the work predicted to take 18 hours will not take even longer? We actually don't know. We do know that now we must get to the root cause of the additional effort.

Based on earned value calculations, the schedule variance for this task at the end of the first week is −7 (hours). (The negative number indicates that the task is behind schedule.)

The Schedule Variance Index (SVI), a measure of productivity, is 68 percent. The best way to interpret the SVI is this: For every hour that is worked, the resource is accomplishing 68 percent of what was expected, or roughly 40 minutes worth of work.

This task is seriously behind schedule. It is only one task, but the implications for the project are important. Some of the questions that should be asked at this point are: Why is this happening? What amount of effort will it take to complete the task? What will the affect be on the rest of the project?

We already know that it will take at least 10 additional hours to complete this task, so what are the implications for other similar tasks? What additional costs will the project incur as a result? According to the estimate in the task description, this task should cost $3,750 (30 hours multiplied by $125). We know is that the actual cost at the end of the first week was $2,750 (22 hours multiplied by $125). We also know that the amount of work actually completed was 15 hours, so the earned value is $1,875 (15 hours multiplied by $125). We calculate the cost variance to be $875, which is over budget.

The Cost Performance Index (CPI), a measure of productivity, would then be $0.68. This means that for each dollar spent on this task, we have achieved a $0.68 return. It follows that this task is 32 percent over budget. When we consider how many tasks there are in a project, it is clear that having even a small percentage of tasks over budget will cause a serious cost overrun. If we apply an estimate-at-completion calculation, we can see that the final cost of the task could be $5,515, rounded to the nearest dollar. This would be $1,765 over budget.

It is clear why it is important to track hours and cost for each task. If completion by a certain date was all we looked at, we would miss the fact that this task is seriously over budget.

Once project managers have determined that there is a variance in project schedule or cost, why it has happened, and what the solution is, they must change the project schedule. Depending on the level of detail that a project is using, this may be done through a schedule change control process or simply by using the project's change control process.

Before making the changes, all of the implications, in particular to overall schedule and costs, must be calculated. Any changes must be approved at the appropriate level of authority, depending on the cost of the change.

CHANGE CONTROL   Rare is the project that does not undergo any changes at all during its full cycle. Projects deal with change, and they themselves are the subjects of frequent change. Change in a project is not bad, but uncontrolled and undocumented change has been the death of many a project. A well-planned project that is not properly controlled will run astray at some point. Change control does not mean that there cannot be any change; it means that change must be regulated with a process to ensure that only those changes that will benefit the project's objectives occur.

A change control process is what prevents changes from drowning the project. The change control process documents all requested changes so that the project team can determine what effect the changes will have in terms of effort and cost. Once the estimates are complete, the stakeholder can accept or reject the change. The key here is that the project manager must have the authority to refuse any change if the stakeholder does not sign off on the effects of the change on the project, on the cost, the resources needed, or the delivery date.

Changes could also affect the financial health of the project. For example, a delay in project execution beyond an agreed-on date or an increase in project scope could require additional resource time. If the additional scope is larger than what was anticipated, it might use all of the contingency time allowed for, increasing the overall project cost. If project cost increases, the return may decrease below the level that is acceptable to the organization. In Chapter 7, we show how change control must be coupled with financial and budget analysis to ensure project health.

RISK CONTROL   Risk control has several facets:

- Monitoring project results for signs that risks may occur or may have occurred
- Reviewing risk responses that have been taken to see if they were effective
- Reviewing project goals and objectives to ensure that they are still valid
- Reviewing the project context to see if there are any changes in external factors that may affect the project

As with all of the other categories of project control, risk control relies on a well-constructed risk plan along with proper execution of the plan. In practical terms, risk monitoring also depends on information gathering to find the information needed to determine whether any risks are either imminent or actually happening.

When gathering and reviewing project information, project managers must make constant reference to the risk plan, which contains information about possible risks, the warning signs that they may happen, and how the risks will be dealt with if they happen. Once the signs of risk appear, project managers initiate the risk response plan and continue to monitor the situation. Finally, project managers evaluate the effectiveness of the response to determine if changes need to be made in the risk plan. The Chapter 7 case study relates risk control to project budget and cash flow.

QUALITY ASSURANCE AND CONTROL   In essence, quality is divided into two facets, quality assurance and quality control. These terms are often confused. In the context of project management, quality assurance refers to project management and quality control refers to the product or service that the project is producing. Quality assurance refers to all of the various activities that are a part of the project's quality.

Project managers monitor quality tasks in the same manner that they monitor all other project tasks: Are they happening on schedule and according to plan? Are quality tasks completed within their allocations of effort and cost? Project quality tasks completed satisfactorily according to plan are not absolute guarantees that quality will be up to par, but they will be an indication that there is a better chance that quality will be present.

Quality control consists of the various tasks within the quality plan that determine whether the project's actual product meets the quality standards that have been set for it. At times general quality standards, such as those of the International Standards Organization, or more specific standards, such as regulations by the Food and Drug Administration in the pharmaceutical industry, are required. At other times, the project team sets the quality standard during the planning process.

In either case, project managers, along with any quality professionals who might be involved, are responsible for ensuring that the quality standards are met. Quality assurance is important because it attempts to ensure that quality is in place before anything is produced; quality control is more focused on testing the results to see that quality standards have been achieved. When quality assurance functions well, it is less likely that there will be problems with quality. When quality control does find that quality standards have not been met, there is usually increased cost for rework. Chapter 4 and Chapter 7 cover the cost of quality.

Status Reporting

Status reporting is the activity that conveys information about project progress to individuals or groups that require information. Status reporting should happen frequently; we suggest weekly or at least once every two weeks. Leaving intervals longer than two weeks creates a risk that problems that occur may go unnoticed and uncorrected for too long a period. This correlates well with the basic duration of a project task: That is usually no more than two weeks.

Project managers are primarily responsible for status reporting, although on larger, more complex projects, an administrator may collect information and report status to the overall project manager, who would then report to other stakeholders as is necessary.

The project status report should be concise and to the point. Depending on the audience, it may have a greater or lesser level of detail. For the project sponsor and anyone else who has a direct stake in the project (including the project team), the status report should be detailed enough so that they will have sufficient information to understand the state of the project and be able to make decisions concerning it. If some issues are more complex, other documents explaining them may accompany the status report. The status report should include at least:

- An accounting of tasks for the period concerned.
- Earned value calculations. If they indicate any problems, any information concerning root causes should be included.

- A financial and accounting dashboard containing pertinent information related to the organization's overall financial and accounting requirements.

Chapters 2 and 3 are about the DuPont Analysis, a manner of analyzing the financial performance of a company. In Chapter 7, we introduce a financial dashboard that will compare project results to the organization's calculations based on the DuPont Analysis.

Notes

1. Kevin Callahan and Lynne Brooks, *The Essentials of Strategic Project Management* (Hoboken, NJ: John Wiley & Sons, 2004).

2. A Guide to the Project Management Body of Knowledge, (Newton Square, PA: Project Management Institute, 2005).

CHAPTER 2

Finance, Strategy, and Strategic Project Management

In Chapter 1, we introduced the idea of how strategy, finance, and project management were interrelated and mapped out how the various phases of project management could be informed by financial analysis. In this chapter we set a foundation of knowledge about how the finances of a business function by introducing the concepts and practice of financial analysis and the tools used to carry them out. We use the financial statements of two companies to illustrate. In Chapter 3, we perform a detailed analysis of a third company, in the context of how to relate that information to project management.

In order to evaluate two or more project alternatives, it is important to know which alternative is a better fit from a strategic and financial perspective. Understanding both of these perspectives depends on how the finances of a company are performing and whether the finances are in good condition. Using different analysis tools, we can become familiar with how well a company is operating.

This chapter emphasizes financial ratio analysis. Don't be worried about the mathematics of financial analysis. The only math you need to know is basic addition, subtraction, multiplication, and division. It is important, however, to learn about certain financial concepts and tools, such as a company balance sheet, income and expense statement, and a financial analysis method called the DuPont Method.

DuPont Method

Let's begin by focusing on the DuPont Method. In academia, financial ratio analysis is often referred to as the DuPont model or method. Its origin stems from the work of an electrical engineer named F. Donaldson Brown, who joined the DuPont Company in 1914. DuPont, then and now, is a giant chemical company. Around the beginning of World War I, DuPont acquired 23 percent of General Motors Corp. (GM). At that time, GM was one of DuPont's largest customers.

General Motors was a huge conglomerate with a quagmire of financial issues. Brown came up with a way of measuring financial performance through the application of financial ratios. This process was the standard for financial managers until the early 1970s. Ratio analysis is still used today, but it has been supplemented with economic value added (EVA) and market value added (MVA) analysis. We discuss EVA and MVA in Chapter 5.

The key highlight on financial ratio analysis is to see how financial operations drive value. Some finance people refer to this model as the value drivers model; others, as the financial levers model. The former see value drivers as the explanation for how an entity makes money and increases its value, hence the term "value driver." The latter view financial ratio analysis as the method for identifying the triggers of financial results, hence the term "financial levers."

The differences between the two models are subtle and arguably an issue of semantics; nevertheless, both schools of thought provide the information that you will need to analyze the financial information and apply it to project management. In this book, we use the term "value driver."

Financial ratio analysis begins with the calculation of financial ratios. Simply put, a financial ratio is essentially taking one number and dividing it by another. The ratios are often grouped according to the type of information that they provide. In this book, we will use profitability, activity, and solvency as groupings for the ratios.

In addition to grouping financial ratios according to the type of information given, there are three different ways of using financial ratio analysis:

1. Cross-company ratio analysis
2. Cross-industry ratio analysis
3. Cross-trend ratio analysis

As the term implies, cross-company analysis is where the financial analyst compares two like businesses. One of the purposes of cross-company analysis is to understand a competitor's weaknesses or strengths. An example would be comparing Coca-Cola to Pepsi. Such an analysis would reveal, for example, that the fundamental business plans of Coca-Cola and Pepsi are very different.

Coca-Cola is a beverage company that sells soft drink syrup to partners that bottle and distribute the beverages. Pepsi, however, is a more diversified company that includes snack foods, restaurants, and other businesses. A cross-company financial analysis would reveal that the types of activities that each company undertakes are somewhat different, and their financial needs are different as well.

A cross-industry analysis entails comparing a company to industry standards. Returning to the example of Coca-Cola, you would compare the company to others in the nonalcoholic beverage industry. You may compare Pepsi to companies that are more diversified than Coca-Cola. This type of analysis helps to understand how the company performs, relative to the industry as a whole.

In cross-trend analysis, you examine financial ratios of a company. This can be done for the purpose of understanding how a company derives value or how the company performs over time. If you have to do cross-company or cross-industry analysis, you will need to seek the help of an accountant familiar with such matters.

To perform cross-trend analysis, you have to be aware of changes in accounting methods from year to year. Generally, accountants issue financial statements for the current period and for the same period in the preceding year. When a change in an accounting method occurs in the current year, the accounting profession requires that the prior periods presented with the current financial statements be restated as if the accounting method had been used at the beginning of that period.

An accounting method is a procedure for recording and reporting a financial transaction. The accounting profession allows for different methods or procedures for reporting financial transactions. As a result, the same transaction (the purchase of materials for manufacturing, for example) can be reported differently by two different companies, resulting in different impacts on their respective financial statements.

When you are working with periods beyond the restated financials, your trend analysis may be distorted by the different accounting methods. We suggest that you seek help from the accounting department in compensating for these differences. Essentially, you should be comparing apples to apples and oranges to oranges. For the remainder of this book, the focus is on cross-trend analysis within a single time period.

DuPont Method Pyramid[1]

Before we introduce the individual ratios and their definitions, let's look at how the ratios relate to one another and how they will reveal a company's financial state. Exhibit 2.1 shows how the essential ratios of a DuPont analysis are broken down. This particular representation, based on an analysis taught by Professor John Affleck-Graves at the University of Notre Dame, contains profitability ratios, activity ratios, and one solvency ratio.

It is important to understand that while each of the ratios stands for a particular piece of financial information, none of the ratios stands on its own. The hierarchy described in Exhibit 2.1 illustrates how the ratio at the top of the pyramid can be decomposed into other ratios. The implication is that if you want to understand what is

EXHIBIT 2.1 DuPont Method in a Pyramid Format

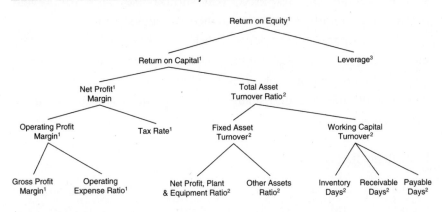

1. Profitability Ratios
2. Activity Ratios
3. Solvency Ratios

happening within a company's finances, you need to look further down the pyramid.

For example, if you would like to understand why return on equity (ROE) is a particular percentage, you would first look at return on capital and leverage. Return on equity is simply return on capital multiplied by leverage. The type of company or industry will have an effect on the ratios as well. If you are analyzing a capital-intense industry, such as manufacturing, inventory days or net profit, plant, and equipment could have a significant effect on ROE. A service company may look more closely at the operating expense ratio. The inverse is also true. If company executives wish to improve their ROE, for example, they will study the ratios that drive value at their company in order to decide what changes they need to make to improve performance. In Chapter 3, we look at examples of how senior project managers must analyze these ratios to understand whether a particular project is actually going to be in alignment with the company's strategy.

All of the ratios that are calculated using a company's balance sheet—which describes the company's assets and liabilities on a particular date—are usually calculated using the year-end balance sheet.

Where averages are required, you should use the current year balance and the preceding year balance and divide by two.

The company's statement of operations, also known as the income and expense statement, provides information for ratios as well. The statement of operations contains information for the year to date. Usually the year-end statement of operations is used for calculating ratios.

Profitability Ratios

Profitability ratios, as the name implies, calculate how much money a business is earning. There are a number of different ways to look at profitability; thus, there is more than one ratio. For example, a company may be generating a large amount of sales or revenue, but the bottom-line profitability may not be what is expected. This could occur because the cost of generating sales or the cost of administration is too high. Using profitability ratios, a determination of where the problem is occurring may be made. Exhibit 2.2 lists examples of the most common profitability ratios.

EXHIBIT 2.2 Profitability Ratios

$$\text{Return on Equity (ROE)} = \frac{\text{Net Income}}{\text{Average Stockholder's Equity}}$$

$$\text{Return on Capital (ROC)} = \frac{\text{Net Income}}{\text{Average of Debt} + \text{Average Stockholder's Equity}}$$

$$\text{Net Profit Margin (NPM)} = \frac{\text{Net Income}}{\text{Sales}}$$

$$\text{Operating Profit Margin (OPM)} = \frac{\text{Income from Operations before Taxes}}{\text{Sales}}$$

$$\text{Tax Rate (TR)} = \frac{\text{Income Taxes}}{\text{Net Income from before Taxes}}$$

$$\text{Gross Profit Margin (GPM)} = \frac{\text{Gross Profit}}{\text{Sales}}$$

$$\text{Operating Expense Ratio (OER)} = \frac{\text{Selling, General, and Administrative Expenses}}{\text{Sales}}$$

Return on equity indicates how much profit was generated by the equity invested in the organization. Equity is all of the value in the company that is not represented by debt. You may have heard the term "financial structure" in reference to a company's debt and equity. A company has assets, such as equipment, cash in the bank, inventory, and others. These assets are financed by debt—what the company owes to outside entities—and by equity—the part that belongs to the owners.

Return on equity indicates the amount of income represented by percentage of the owner's investment in a year. For example, a company that has a 20 percent ROE indicates that for every $100 invested, the company made $20 ($100 × 20% = $20). ROE is calculated by dividing the company's net income by the average stockholders equity. (Whenever we use the term "average" for a ratio, we mean that the formula is using an average based on the beginning and the end-of-year figures. Using an average figure compensates for any changes during the year.) The fortunes and futures of many executives have risen and fallen with a company's ROE.

The next ratio is return on capital (ROC). It indicates the percentage of an organization's net income generated relative to the amount of capital that a company possesses. Capital can be defined as the combined assets of a company, and is always equal to the amount of debt and equity that the company maintains. The formula for calculating ROC is:

$$\text{Net Income}/\text{Average Debt} + \text{Equity (capital)}$$

We can look at this in a similar manner to ROE: If $100 of capital returns $15, then we would say that ROC is 15 percent.

You may ask what the difference between ROE and ROC is—a good question! If you refer to Exhibit 2.1, ROE contains both ROC and leverage. We define leverage more fully later. ROE only explains what return investors receive on the equity that they have invested in the company. ROC explains how much, in terms of a percentage, the company returns on invested capital, which is financed by both debt and equity. Leverage, the ratio of debt to equity, can have a significant impact on the overall profitability of a company. We explain this more fully when we talk about solvency ratios.

Net profit margin (NPM) is the primary profitability ratio that indicates the percentage of each dollar of sales remaining after paying all the costs and income taxes. This is the company's bottom line. This ratio is defined as net income divided by sales. NPM tells a story, but it is a high-level story. At times, you will have to dig deeper into the profitability ratios to understand the full story.

Operating profit margin (OPM) (not to be confused with other people's money) indicates the percentage of each dollar of sales that remains after paying for all expenses with the exception of income taxes. As we mentioned, a company may be generating great sales figures, but if operating the firm costs too much, then profits will be low. OPM can indicate when operations are too expensive. The formula for OPM is:

Income from Operations before Taxes/Sales

As the formula indicates, taxes are not considered an operating expense.

The tax rate (TR) indicates the percentage of each dollar of profit owed to the organization's respective taxing authorities. The formula for TR is:

Income Taxes/Net Income before Income Taxes

Gross profit margin (GPM) indicates the percentage of profit derived on each dollar of sales after paying for the cost of the sale but before operating expenses, interest expense, and income taxes. GPM helps us to differentiate between expenses that are incurred to produce a sale, such as the cost of manufacturing a product or the cost of an employee who provides a service, from the cost of running the company, or overhead.

If net profit is not up to expectations, the cause could be too high a cost of producing the sale. The formula for calculating GPM is:

Gross Profit/Sales

Operating expense ratio (OER) indicates the percentage of each dollar of sales used to pay for the organization's selling, general, and administrative expenses. This ratio considers the company's operating expenses that are not addressed in GPM, indicating what it costs to run the company, including the cost of sales and marketing as well as the cost of administering the company. The formula for OER is:

Selling, General, and Administrative Expenses/Sales

Note the difference between the cost of selling and the cost of sales. Cost of sales is the cost to make a product or provide a service. It can be attributed directly to the product or service sold. Selling is a general expense the company incurs, such as advertising, which cannot be attributed directly to the production of the product or service. We cover this topic more fully in Chapter 4.

Activity Ratios

The next financial ratios to be familiar with are the activity ratios, which measure the amount of assets needed to support operations. It is sometimes said that "It takes money to make money." Although the activity ratios don't specifically measure money, they do measure the monetary equivalents of the assets that are needed to allow a company to operate. Remember, assets can be fixed, such as the plant and equipment that are needed to manufacture products, or they can be nonfixed, such as the inventory that is kept on hand to meet variations in consumer demand. In a services company, fixed assets could be the offices and equipment that employees use to provide services (see Exhibit 2.3).

The primary activity ratio is the total asset turnover ratio (TATR). This ratio indicates the frequency that sales or revenues cycle in proportion to the amount of assets deployed. Another way to look at this ratio would be to ask how many times is a dollar's worth of assets used to create a dollar's worth of sales. If your company has $1,000 of

EXHIBIT 2.3 Activity Ratios

$$\text{Total Asset Turnover Ratio (TATR)} = \frac{\text{Sales}}{\text{Average Total Assets}}$$

$$\text{Fixed Asset Turnover Ratio (FATR)} = \frac{\text{Sales}}{\text{Average Fixed Assets}}$$

$$\frac{\text{Net Property, Plant, and}}{\text{Equipment Ratio (NPPER)}} = \frac{\text{Sales}}{\text{Average Net Property, Plant, and Equipment}}$$

$$\text{Other Asset Ratio (OAR)} = \frac{\text{Sales}}{\text{Average Other Assets}}$$

$$\frac{\text{Working Capital}}{\text{Ratio (WCR)}} = \frac{\text{Sales}}{\text{Average Current Assets} - \text{Average Current Liabilities}}$$

$$\text{Inventory Turnover Ratio (ITR)} = \frac{\text{Cost of Goods Sold}}{\text{Average Inventory}}$$

$$\text{Days of Inventory on Hand (DIOH)} = \frac{\text{Average Inventory}}{\text{Cost of Goods Sold}/365}$$

$$\text{Accounts Receivable Collection Period} = \frac{\text{Average Accounts Receivable}}{\text{Credit Sales}/365}$$

$$\text{Accounts Payable Collection Period} = \frac{\text{Average Accounts Payable}}{\text{Credit Sales}/365}$$

assets and sales of $2,000, you would say that the TATR is 2. In other words, you have used that $1,000 of assets twice to create $1,000 worth of sales. The higher this ratio, the more efficiently the company is using the assets. The formula for TATR is:

Sales/Total Average Assets

Fixed asset turnover ratio (FATO) indicates how efficient an organization is at generating sales given its level of fixed assets. As we mentioned, fixed assets are things such as plant, equipment, and offices. The FATO is particularly important in manufacturing, as it indicates how well the firm is using assets to produce sales; the higher the ratio, the more efficient the operation. The formula for FATO is:

Sales/Average Fixed Assets

Net property, plant, and equipment ratio (NPPER) indicates the percentage of depreciated property, plant, and equipment (PPE) required to generate one dollar of sales. Each year the PPE used in a business is depreciated to show its decreasing value over time. The term "fixed assets" indicates the total value of all assets; NPPER only shows the efficiency of depreciated assets. The formula for NPPER is:

Sales/Average Net Property, Plant, and Equipment

Other asset ratio (OAR) indicates the percentage of other assets needed to generate one dollar of sales. The OAR is defined in equation format as:

Sales/Average Other Assets

Working capital ratio (WCR) indicates how much money, in terms of a percentage of each dollar of a sale, an organization requires to generate that sale. Working capital is the amount of money that the company has invested in current assets less current liabilities. For example, a current asset would be accounts receivable (the money that the company is owed for products delivered or services rendered). In essence, accounts receivable is like a no-interest loan to the customer, and represents an investment that the company must use to cover the cost of producing the product or delivering the service before it is paid by the customer.

Accounts payable, however, is like a no-interest loan from the vendors that provide products and services to the company. A vendor may be the supplier of raw materials to a manufacturer. A company would always like to minimize receivables and maximize payables. One reason why a company might have very good sales but be cash-poor could be that account receivables are too slow in coming in. This ratio indicates the level of investment the company has made to keep operations going. The formula for working capital is:

Sales/Average Current Assets − Average Current Liabilities

Inventory turnover ratio (ITO) indicates how efficiently an organization cycles its inventory in a given year. In other words, how many times does the company replace the inventory on hand with new inventory? A higher ITO indicates that the company is operating more efficiently and is able to meet fluctuations in demand without keeping excessive amounts of inventory on hand. The formula for ITO is:

Cost of Goods Sold/Average Inventory

Note that sales does not appear in this ratio (because it reflects the cost to the company and not the value when sold). Inventory is valued at its cost before being sold.

Inside of the activity ratio grouping are the cash cycle ratios. Cash cycle ratios consider the cost of annual expenses, including cost of goods sold, broken down to the amount per day. The results of the calculation indicate how many days of cash are needed to run the business.

The first cash cycle ratio we'll discuss is days of inventory on hand (DOIOH). This ratio indicates the number of days it will take for your inventory on hand to run out. Achieving a balance between having enough inventory on hand to meet demand and not risking losses by having too much inventory is the goal. The formula for DOIOH is:

Average Inventory/(Quotient of Cost of Goods Sold/365)

Accounts receivable collection period indicates the number of days it takes to collect a credit sale. As mentioned, accounts receivable is like a non-interest loan to the customer. The formula for accounts receivable collection period is:

Average Accounts Receivable/(Quotient of Credit Sales/365)

We should note that, with the exception of retail companies, most companies' sales are credit sales.

Accounts payable collection period indicates the number of days in which you pay for your credit purchases. The formula for accounts payable collection period is:

Average Accounts Payable/(Quotient of Credit Sales/365)

Solvency Ratios

The last financial ratios are referred to as solvency ratios. These ratios are used to determine how leveraged and/or solvent the business is. Earlier we discussed the financial structure of a company. You will recall that "financial structure" refers to the proportion of debt and equity that the company maintains. Changes in these proportions can have an effect on the company's finances (see Exhibit 2.4).

The primary ratio in this grouping is the leverage multiplier (LM), which is also simply called leverage. The LM indicates the ratio of equity to the total assets or capital. The formula for leverage is:

$$\text{Average Total Assets/Average Total Equity}$$

Although it is not mentioned in the formula, debt has an effect on leverage.

If the amount of assets in a company rises, and equity does not rise with it, then debt must rise (remember: Assets = Debt + Equity!). We often hear that increasing debt is not a good thing. However, when a company is working efficiently to make a good return,

EXHIBIT 2.4 Solvency Ratios

$$\text{Leverage (LM)} = \frac{\text{Average Total Assets}}{\text{Average Total Equity}}$$

$$\text{Debt to Equity Ratio (D2E)} = \frac{\text{Average Total Debt}}{\text{Average Stockholder's Equity}}$$

$$\text{Debt to Equity Asset (D2A)} = \frac{\text{Average Total Debt}}{\text{Average Total Assets}}$$

$$\text{Times Interest Earned Ratio (TIE)} = \frac{\text{Earnings Before Interest and Taxes}}{\text{Interest Expense}}$$

$$\text{Times Burden Covered Ratio (TBCR)} = \frac{\text{Earnings Before Interest and Taxes}}{\text{Interest} + (\text{Principal Repayment}/1 - \text{Tax Rate})}$$

$$\text{Current Ratio} = \frac{\text{Average Current Assets}}{\text{Average Current Liabilities}}$$

$$\text{Quick Ratio} = \frac{\text{Average Current Assets} - \text{Average Inventory}}{\text{Average Current Liabilities}}$$

increasing the amount of business done by increasing debt can actually increase ROE.

As an example, a company has $3,000 in total average assets, of which $2,000 is average equity (meaning that debt is $1,000). The Leverage Multiplier would be $3,000 divided by $2,000, or 1.5. If return on capital is 10 percent (i.e., 10 cents on each dollar of capital invested), and leverage is 1.5, then ROE is 10 percent multiplied by 1.5, or 15 percent. So leverage helps the company return 15 percent on a dollar of invested equity.

Let's say that average total assets in the company are increased to $4,000, but total equity stays the same. That means that debt has now risen by $1,000. Leverage is now calculated as $4,000 divided by $2,000, or 2. If we multiply the ROC (10 percent) by 2, we now have an ROE of 20 percent. Increasing debt allowed the company to increase ROE by 5 percent. The cautionary note here is to be sure the company can keep its ROC at the same rate in order to achieve better results while expanding operations (whether financed by debt or equity).

One of the more common solvency ratios is the debt to equity (D2E) ratio. The D2E indicates to what degree an organization is financed with debt. The formula for D2E is:

Average Total Debt/Average Stockholder's Equity

In the previous example, the D2E before the increase would be $1,000 divided by $2,000, or 50 percent. After the increase, the ratio would be $2,000 divided by $2,000, or 100 percent.

The complement ratio to the debt to equity ratio is the debt to assets (D2A) ratio. The formula for the D2A ratio is:

Average Total Debt/Average Total Assets

The times interest earned (TIE) ratio is also referred to as a coverage ratio. It indicates how many times an organization can pay its annual interest expense burden out of earnings before interest and taxes (EBIT). By calculating the TIE ratio with EBIT, we learn how well the company can cope with debt, after it has paid for other expenses (cost of sales, selling, and general and administration costs). In this day of mergers, this is an important ratio to study. If a company takes on too much debt, it may not be able to cover its interest expenses out of earnings (not to mention repayment of capital). The formula for TIE is:

Earnings before Interest and Taxes/Interest Expense

Times burden covered ratio (TBCR) is similar to the TIE ratio, but it also takes into account the principal paydown of debt. In the banking community, TBCR is referred to as debt service cover ratio (DSCR). The formula for the TIE ratio is:

Earnings before Interest and Taxes/Interest +
(Quotient of Principal/1 − Tax Rate)

The effect of dividing the principal repayment by 1 minus the tax rate is to remove the effect of tax deductions from consideration.

Practical Application of Ratios

The formula for ROE is net income divided by average stockholders' equity. In Exhibit 2.5, the net income for Pontrelli Recycling Inc. for 2005 is $1,681,483. Since it is a line item on the statement of operations, you don't need to use an average. Because stockholders' equity is a line item on the balance sheet, you need to calculate the annual average.

In Exhibit 2.5, stockholders' equity for December 31, 2005, and 2004 are $4,736,649 and $ 3,055,166, respectively. The average of these two numbers is $3,895,908 [($4,736,649 + $3,055,166)/2]. Following the formula, ROE in 2005 for Pontrelli Recycling Inc. was 43.2 percent ($1,681,483/$3,895,908).

Exhibits 2.5 and 2.6 are for demonstrating how to use financial ratio analysis. They represent summarized financial information on two different types of businesses. Pontrelli Recycling, Inc. is a ferrous and nonferrous metal recycling business with inventory and cost of goods sold. Patrick J. Romano Jr., P.C., is a single-attorney law

EXHIBIT 2.5 Pontrelli Recycling, Inc. Balance Sheet and
Statement of Operations

Pontrelli recycling, Inc.
Balance Sheet

	December 31, 2010	December 31, 2009
Cash	$ 3,450,000	$ 2,254,815
Accounts Receivable	$ 1,645,827	$ 564,532
Inventory	$ 1,153,515	$ 1,331,940
Total Current Assets	$ 6,249,342	$ 4,151,287
Net Property, Plant, and Equip.	$ 214,119	$ 369,116
Other Assets	$ 188,482	$ 211,190
Total Assets	$ 6,651,943	$ 4,731,593
Accounts Payable	$ 259,663	$ 27,246
Notes Payable—Short Term	$ 440,318	$ 425,786
Payroll and Sales Tax Payable	$ 85,374	$ 1,490
State Income Taxes Payable	$ 711	$ -0-
Total Current Liabilities	$ 786,066	$ 454,522
Notes Payable—Long Term	$ 1,129,228	$ 1,221,905
Total Liabilities	$ 1,915,294	$ 1,676,427
Stockholders' Equity	$ 4,736,649	$ 3,055,166
Total Liabilities and Stockholders' Equity	$ 6,651,943	$ 4,731,593

EXHIBIT 2.5 (*Continued*)

Pontrelli Recycling, Inc.
Statement of Operations
For the Year Ending

	2010	2009
Sales	$ 36,957,183	$ 32,751,694
Cost Of Sales	$ 31,552,817	$ 28,273,539
Gross Profit	$ 5,404,366	$ 4,478,155
Selling, Administrative, and General Expenses (Operating Expenses)	$ 2,459,287	$ 2,541,286
Income From Operations	$ 2,945,079	$ 1,936,869
Interest Expense	$ 142,608	$ 129,398
Income Before Taxes	$ 2,802,471	$ 1,807,471
Income Taxes	$ 1,120,988	$ 722,988
Net Income	$ 1,681,483	$ 1,084,483

practice, which is categorized as a service business. The summarized financial data is that of two actual businesses. To protect the companies' privacy, the names have been changed and some adjustments have been made to the financials.

Exhibit 2.7 is the result of applying the financial ratio formulas to the information in Exhibits 2.5 and 2.6. While reading through the discussion on financial ratios, you may have noticed that the formulas are similar and that in some cases the denominators and numerators flip back and forth. Without getting into a heavy discussion of mathematics, this interchanging of denominators and numerators creates distinct mathematical relationships between the financial ratios. The relationship among the ratios is the foundation for financial ratio analysis.

As indicated earlier, financial ratio analysis begins with ROE, and there are three groupings of ratios: profitability ratios, activity ratios, and solvency ratios. Now get ready for the revelation: When you multiply the primary profitability ratio (net profit margin) by the primary activity ratio (total asset turnover rate) and then multiply that product by the primary solvency ratio (leverage multiplier), the resulting

EXHIBIT 2.6 Patrick J. Romano, Jr., P.C. Balance Sheet and Statement of Operations

Patrick J. Romano, Jr., P.C.
Balance Sheet

	December 31, 2010	December 31, 2009
Cash	$ 7,776	$ 1,813
Accounts Receivable	$ 180,408	$ 69,796
Total Current Assets	$ 188,184	$ 71,609
Net Property, Plant, and Equip.	$ 4,486	$ 9,293
Total Assets	$ 192,670	$ 86,152
Accounts Payable	$ 30,654	$ 29,250
Payroll Taxes Payable	$ 1,910	$ 11,038
Income Taxes Payable	$ 31,685	$ 8,236
Note Payable—Short Term	$ -0-	$ 33,412
Total Current Liabilities	$ 64,249	$ 81,936
Total Long Term Liabilities	$ -0-	$ -0-
Total Liabilities	$ 64,249	$ 81,936
Stockholder's Equity	$ 128,421	$ 4,216
Total Liabilities and Stockholder's Equity	$ 192,670	$ 86,152

EXHIBIT 2.6 (*Continued*)

Patrick J. Romano, Jr., P.C.
Statement of Operations
For the Year Ending

	2010	2009
Fee Income	$ 1,014,078	$ 879,406
Operating Expenses	$ 825,770	$ 842,558
Operating Income	$ 188,308	$ 36,848
Interest Expense	$ 118	$ 2,533
Income Before Taxes	$ 188,190	$ 34,315
Income Taxes	$ 63,985	$ 8,236
Net Income	$ 124,205	$ 26,079

product will equal the return on equity calculation (NPM × TATR × LM = ROE).

For example, the 2005 return on equity for Pontrelli Recycling Inc. was 43.2 percent. The net profit margin percentage, total asset turnover ratio, and the leverage multiplier were 4.5 percent, 6.5 percent, and 1.46 percent, respectively, for the year ending 2005. Plugging these into the formula gives us:

$$4.5\% \times 6.5 \times 1.46 = \text{approximately } 43\%$$

Note that the calculated value isn't exactly equal to the ROE percentage. This is a very important issue and something you must always remember. The values aren't exactly equal due to rounding.

Typically, when the DuPont Method is taught, students are given hypothetical financial statements that use nice round numbers whose ratios are finite to one or two decimal places. Hence, the ROE and the calculation of the primary ratios are equal. The examples in Exhibits 2.5 and 2.6 were chosen specifically because both businesses have very unsymmetrical numbers. As you calculate the ratios to a

EXHIBIT 2.7 Calculated Financial Ratios

	Pontrelli Recycling, Inc.	Patrick J. Romano, Jr., P.C.
Profitability Ratios		
ROE	43.2%	187.3%
ROC	29.5%	89.1%
NPM	4.5%	12.2%
OPM	7.6%	18.6%
TR	39.9%	34.0%
GPM	14.6%	N/A
OER	6.7%	81.4%
Activity Ratios		
TATR	6.5	7.3
FATO	127	147
NPPER	127	147
OAR	185	N/A
WCR	8.06	17.9
ITO	25.40	N/A
DOIOH	14 days	N/A
ARCP	11 days	45 days
APCP	2 days	N/A
Solvency Ratios		
LM	1.46	2.10
D2E	0.46	1.10
D2A	0.32	0.52
TIE	20.65	1596.00
TBCR	10.50	3.71
CR	8.38	1.77
QR	6.38	1.77

greater number of decimal places, the calculated value of the primary ratios and the actual calculation of ROE get closer to being equal. Also note that your calculations don't have to be to the tenth decimal place in order for financial ratio analysis to work.

EXHIBIT 2.8 DuPont Method Traditional Worksheet Template

	Profitability Ratios			
	GPM			
		OPM		
			NPM	
		TR		
	OER			
	Activity Ratios			
	FATO			
	OAR		TATR	
	NPPER			
DOIOH	ITO			
ARCP				
APCP	WCR			
				ROE
	Solvency Ratios			
TIE				
TBCR		D2E		
			LM	
CR		D2A		
QR				

Getting back to the DuPont Method, each primary ratio of the three groupings has secondary ratios that manifest themselves in the primary ratios. The secondary ratios then have subsidiary ratios that are manifested within them. This reductive process of starting with ROE and removing the layers that drive you down to price and the cash cycle is what the method is all about. Exhibit 2.8 is an example of what a finance person's worksheet might look like.

You can choose the Pyramid format or the Traditional Worksheet format, whichever you are the most comfortable with. Keep in mind that one of the attributes of the DuPont Method is that it is a reductive process. In other words, the exercise starts with the big picture and keeps peeling the layers back until you find what you are looking for. By starting at the top, as shown in Exhibit 2.1, the reductive process becomes more intuitive. In Exhibit 2.8 you start from the right and proceed to the left through the worksheet, filling in the actual numbers next to the ratio names or acronyms. In addition, the number crunching ends once you have found the value driver or the financial lever that you are looking for.

In the next chapter, we will continue our work with ratios and the DuPont Method when we analyze the finances of a mythical food company to "understand" where the company is having troubles and to decide on what must be done to improve its financial picture.

Note

1. As presented by John Affleck-Graves, professor of economics at the University of Notre Dame, Mendoza College.

CHAPTER 3

Accounting, Finance, and Project Management

In Chapter 2, we defined the DuPont Method for analyzing a company's finances. In this chapter, we apply that method to the financials of a mythical company, although the figures are based on a real company. Our emphasis during this analysis is in identifying information that is important for project managers and team members to know.

Why is there a link among accounting, finance, and project management? The answer is not complex: If all members of a project team do not understand how they are carrying forward the company's mission and strategy with the project that they are working on, and in particular each employee's part in the project, then the project has a good chance of going awry. That understanding includes how the project contributes to the value of the company in a very concrete way and how each individual on the project team is a part of the contribution.

As we pointed out in Chapter 1, the strategy of a company must be driven by financials; whatever the company's mission is, without sound financials, the company cannot succeed. The DuPont financial analysis allows us to take a close look at a company's finances and determine the current situation as well as study how things could be manipulated to improve the financial picture. The value drivers or levers that are represented by the different financial ratios give a company the ability to change its financial performance. The ability to identify the levers and how to manipulate them needs to be well known at all levels of a company.

Project Team and Financial Success

In this chapter, we first review a case study of how strategic project management can help a company link project success to financial success and motivate the project team to be successful by having them understand how they will affect the company's (and possibly their own) finances. In the case study, we use financial and accounting information to discover where the real problems are with the company's finances and discuss some implications of different solutions.

In Chapter 7, a second case study presents the problems of another company and how project management and accounting and finance work together to ensure that projects are executed properly and contribute to the company's well-being.

In the second part of this chapter, we show how the implementation of strategic project management will help a company to forge a link between company mission and objectives, strategy, and everyday project work.

In order to illustrate how important the link is, let's take a look at an example of a fictitious food manufacturing company that is not performing well (see Exhibit 3.1). Marvelous Food's mission is to provide customers with delicious products that are healthy and nutritious. At the same time, Marvelous Food wishes to give investors a good return on their investment. Unfortunately, that is not happening. To see why that is not happening, we can break down Marvelous Food's financials using a DuPont analysis. All of the information in Exhibit 3.1 is calculated based on Marvelous Food's balance sheet (Exhibit 3.2) and income and expense statement (Exhibit 3.3).

First of all, we look at return on equity (ROE), the return that the company makes on each dollar of equity that is invested in the firm. In the case of Marvelous Food, the ROE is 17.55 percent. The industry

EXHIBIT 3.1 Marvelous Food Inc. Ratios*

	Marvelous	Industry
Profitability Ratios		
Return on Equity	17.55%	33.7%
Return on Capital	11.67%	12.5%
Net Profit Margin	12.2%	5.6%
Operating Profit Margin	17.99%	26.1%
Tax Rate	32.15%	19.4%
Gross Profit Margin	38.67%	40.3%
Operating Expense Ratio	18.87%	26.8%
Activity Ratios		
Total Asset Turnover Ratio	0.96	2.2
Fixed Asset Turnover Ratio	3.62	8.5
Working Capital Ratio	1.95	6.0
Inventory Turnover Ratio	1.27	8.4
Days of Inventory on Hand	287.4	43.7
Accounts Receivable Collection Period	72.8	22.3
Accounts Payable Collection Period	11.9	14.8
Solvency Ratios		
Leverage	1.5	2.7
Debt to Equity	0.5	1.7
Times Interest Earned Ratio	10.94	3.0
Current Ratio	3.82	1.5
Quick Ratio	1.17	0.9

*Industry information from BizMiner © 1998–2006, The Brandon Company.

average for the food industry is 33.7 percent; thus, Marvelous Food is significantly below the industry average. To understand why Marvelous Food is below the industry average, let's follow the DuPont analysis down into more detail.

ROE is made up of return on capital (total asset turnover) and leverage. Leverage is the amount of debt that Marvelous Food has in proportion to its equity. This is multiplied by the company's return on capital, which is what Marvelous Food returned on each dollar of

EXHIBIT 3.2 Marvelous Food Inc. Balance Sheet

December 31	2010	2009
Assets		
Cash & Equivalents	$ 67,183	$ 54,837
Accounts Receivable	$ 1,110,578	$ 817,860
Inventory	$ 2,441,136	$ 2,228,720
Total Current Assets	$ 3,618,897	$ 3,101,417
Property, Plant, and Equipment, Net	$ 1,327,310	$ 1,346,158
Other Assets	$ 597,194	$ 125,333
Total Assets	$ 5,543,401	$ 4,572,908
Liabilities		
Accounts Payable	$ 167,812	$ 148,686
Short Term Debt	$ 819,059	$ 343,277
Current Portion of Long Term Debt	$ 56	$ 279,043
Total Current Liabilities	$ 986,927	$ 771,006
Long Term Debt	$ 942,755	$ 690,602
Total Liabilities	$ 1,929,682	$ 1,461,608
Stockholder's Equity	$ 3,613,719	$ 3,111,300
Total Liabilities and Stockholder's Equity	**$5,543,401**	**$4,572,908**

capital that it used to move the company forward. In this case, Marvelous Food has a return on capital of 11.67 percent and leverage of 1.50. Our second clue is that the return on capital is also below the industry average of 12.5 percent. We must follow this clue further into Marvelous Food's finances.

Return on capital is made up of net profit margin (what is left after all expenses are accounted for) and capital turnover (how many times each dollar of capital is used during the year, also known as total asset turnover). Here we begin to see why we may need to follow the DuPont analysis all the way to the bottom of the pyramid to understand the real problem. Net profit margin, at 12.20 percent, is slightly above the industry average of 5.6 percent. We might be

EXHIBIT 3.3 Marvelous Food Inc. Income and Expense Statement

December 31	2010	2009
Sales	$4,835,000	$4,429,000
Cost of Sales	$2,965,540	$2,680,437
Gross Profit	$1,869,460	$1,748,563
Selling and General Administrative	$ 912,250	$ 867,104
Income before Interest and Taxes	$ 957,210	$ 881,459
Intesest Expense	$ 87,500	$ 65,525
Income Before Taxes	$ 869,710	$ 815,934
Taxes	$ 279,650	$ 237,237
Net Income	**$ 590,060**	**$ 578,697**

tempted to think all is well until we see that capital turnover at 0.96 is well below the industry average of 2.2.

What these statistics mean is that capital is stuck somewhere within the business cycle and not circulating as well as it should. In the food industry, capital turnover is crucial; profit margins on individual products are not high, so companies must maintain a high volume of production and sales to meet profit targets. Marvelous Food is not maintaining a high rate of turnover.

Capital turnover, which consists of fixed assets turnover multiplied by working capital turnover, is a more complex issue. As we have seen, fixed assets turnover tells us how well we are using the plant and equipment that Marvelous Food maintains, while working capital turnover divided by sales tells us how well we are using the company's liquid assets. In the case of Marvelous Food, we are getting closer to finding our problem. Fixed assets turnover, at 3.62, is below the industry average of 8.5, as is working capital turnover, at 1.95, compared to the average of 6.0.

When we analyze working capital turnover, we find the culprit, or culprits, so to speak. Days of inventory on hand (the amount of inventory that is kept on hand) at Marvelous Food is 287. That is well over the industry average of 45. In addition, the accounts payable collection period (the number of days that the company must wait to be paid by customers) is 72.8, well above the industry average of 22.3. Now we know that Marvelous Food is, in a sense, locking away its value by keeping too much inventory on hand. It is adding to the problem by waiting so long to be paid by customers.

To summarize, the DuPont analysis of Marvelous Food reveals three problems:

1. The company is not using its plants and equipment in an efficient way.
2. It is maintaining a high level of inventory that is very costly.
3. Marvelous Food is taking too long to collect what other companies owe it.

Yet Marvelous Food does show some positive signs. At 12.2 percent, its net profit margin is above the industry average compared to the average of 5.6 percent. Leverage is below the industry average, meaning that Marvelous Food is not saddled with debt compared to equity.

Now that we know what the problem is from a financial point of view, we can analyze the effect of solutions on Marvelous Food's financial picture. We know that by making improvements that adjust the levers of days of inventory on hand and accounts payable collection days, for example, we can affect the company's financial performance overall.

Note that we have not yet found the solution, but we have found the effect that the solution must have in order to improve Marvelous Food's financial performance. Now the company must figure out how to make changes in order to cause the proper financial effect. Once the company's executives decide on a course of action, senior management can plan the steps that must be taken to change course. Those steps, according to our definition, constitute the strategy of Marvelous Food.

Why do project managers need to understand how to analyze company finances? It seems like a lot of detail that does not concern them. The answer is that project managers need to understand company finances in order to ensure that the solution fits the problem and will actually deliver improved results to the company.

Say Marvelous Food decides to improve its ROE to 20 percent and that the strategy for doing so is to decrease both days of inventory on hand and accounts receivable collection period, while maintaining the level of equity in the company. The intended effect will be to improve capital turnover by improving working capital turnover, thereby improving return on capital and return on equity.

Improving Marvelous Food's finances by decreasing both days of inventory on hand and accounts receivable collection period is about improving ROE. In other words, we have a project or in this case a number of projects that appear to be crucial to the financial health of Marvelous Food. The project manager must be able to make the link between the strategic need, improved financial performance, and the deliverables that the project will produce in order for Marvelous Food's employees to understand and accept that change.

Often projects are initiated without the deliverables being properly defined. In the early stages, the deliverables must answer the business needs expressed, but do not have to be so concrete as to set the project off in the wrong direction without the possibility of change. In the case of Marvelous Food, the business need is to improve financial performance by lowering days of inventory on hand and accounts receivable collection period. Some might jump to the conclusion that Marvelous Food needs a new inventory or accounting software system. Others might say that Marvelous Food must rework its supply chain or undergo business process reengineering.

By insisting that the proposed solution be grounded in real research, the project manager will be able to see when people are jumping to conclusions. This does not mean that the project manager must be an expert in supply chain or accounting software processes. The project manager does need to understand how the implementation of any proposed solution will affect the business need.

In the case of Marvelous Food, the project manager must understand enough about how the company's finances work so as to be able to judge what the effect of any proposed solution will actually be.

Knowledge of how company finances work combined with project management methodology and tools will enable the project manager to add value by ensuring that the projects proposed are the right projects and that they will deliver the results that correspond to the actual business need. In particular, a project charter, project budget, and project schedule, along with net present value, internal rate of return, and cost of capital calculations will greatly assist the project manager in determining the proper project choices. Using these tools, let's analyze Marvelous Food's options.

Let us begin with the project charter, a tool that is used in the initiation of projects.[1] A project charter poses several questions that are pertinent to Marvelous Food's situation:

- Define the business needs that the project addresses.
- What are the high-level deliverables?
- Has a financial analysis been done?
- What constitutes project success?
- How will project success be measured?

The business need that is being addressed is that Marvelous Food's financials, specifically return on equity and return on capital, are below industry standards. The executives of Marvelous Food have decided that over the next two years, they wish to return Marvelous Food to industry standard levels and in subsequent years to continue to meet or surpass industry standards for these financial measures.

At this point, it would be a mistake to define high-level deliverables too concretely. Actually, in most cases, the first phase of the project ought to be research into the root causes of the problem and the development of proposals to correct the problem. Often companies will conduct inadequate research into a solution or skip this phase completely. We do not want to advocate moving too quickly, but for the sake of our example, let's say that Marvelous

Food has already carried out the research phase, and we will study the resulting proposal.

The high-level deliverables proposed to solve the financial problems at Marvelous Food are:

- A new supply chain process and tool that will enable Marvelous Food to better anticipate customer demand and thereby reduce inventory and time production to demand
- A revised inventory tracking system integrated into the supply chain system
- A new accounts receivable policy process to collect receivables more quickly and efficiently

In addition to the high-level deliverables, Marvelous Food has obtained several proposals from outside vendors and conducted project planning. Now the company can study the results to see not only the potential improvement that the new processes and systems may bring, but also what the cost to the company will be.

At this point in the life of a project or a program, often project managers are not part of the decision-making process. In many cases, it is because the project manager is not believed to have the business experience necessary to make such decisions. However, using the project management and business tools mentioned earlier, a project manager can guide the decision process to avoid making costly mistakes. It will not always be easy for project managers to have input into important financial decisions, but without some knowledge of how finance and strategy work, they will have no input at all.

Calculating Return on Investment

When planning for new projects or programs, we often hear senior management and executives asking about Return on Investment (ROI). Return on Investment is a very general term that can mean many different things. Often it seems to mean "How long will it be before we earn back what we have invested, and how much more will we earn than we invested?"

When we analyze that definition of ROI, we can see that it leaves out crucial questions: What is the source of the funding to do the project, working capital or debt? What is the cost of raising that capital? What is the length and timing of the cash outflow? When will the cash inflow begin, in what amounts and frequency, and how long will it last? What effects will the cash flow have on company finances? Finally, how risky is the project?

In order to calculate the effects of a project in order to improve financial returns, we must know what the costs of the project will be, as well as the projected benefits to revenue. Let us assume that the cost of the project includes software: Supply chain and accounts receivable tools that will cost $500,000, while implementation costs for software will be an additional $750,000. Reengineering the supply chain and accounts receivable processes is estimated to cost another $1,500,000 for consulting assistance. In addition, the cost of Marvelous Food's employee work on the project will be about $450,000, for an estimated project total of $3,250,000. It is estimated that re-engineering the supply chain process will take six months, with another six months to implement the new process and tools.

Equity or Debt?

First of all, what will be the source of funding? Will Marvelous Food fund the project out of working capital, cash reserves, or by taking on more debt? What effect will this decision have on Marvelous Food's finances?

At the present time, Marvelous Food has a working capital of $2,632,026 including $1,110,578 in accounts receivable, $2,441,136 in inventory, and $67,183 in cash reserves. In addition, Marvelous Food's long-term debt is $942,755 at an average interest rate of 9.3 percent. At first glance, it may seem to be a good idea to use working capital to finance the project. However, part of Marvelous Food's problem is a lack of liquidity because it has large amounts of cash tied up in inventory and accounts receivable. The objective of the project is to correct that imbalance. The only real choice for Marvelous Food is debt.

Exhibit 3.4 illustrates the cash outflows of the project. Technically, the benefits of the project are not cash inflows, but the money saved by the new processes have the same effect as increasing the cash inflows, so we will analyze the savings as if they were cash inflows.

The cash outflows from the project actually begin during the first month of the project, March, with the start of process reengineering. In August, the software vendor and consultant require a 20 percent down payment to reserve resources and begin work on the implementation of the new software tools. During the project, there are additional payments to be made as various milestones are met, roughly every month for the duration of the project.

The project is expected to last for 12 months; therefore, the monthly cash outflow will vary between $250,000 for the first month, as high as $600,000 at mid-project, and then between $200,000 and $250,000 for the balance of the project. Since the payments are timed on the completion of specific deliverables, the payment schedule could vary.

Given that the project is occurring over the course of a year, at least, we cannot say that the cost of the project is exactly equal to the cash outflows. Since the money for the project is raised through additional debt, the cost of that debt must be calculated. Chapter 5 gives a thorough explanation of debt financing of projects.

If the project had been funded by working capital or cash reserves, then Marvelous Food's weighted average cost of capital (WACC) would also be used to calculate the cost. Chapter 5 provides an explanation of WACC and its use in project financing.

We do not expect any cash inflow from the project in the first year, but during the second year, we expect to reduce both average days of inventory on hand and average receivable days. The results

EXHIBIT 3.4 Marvelous Food's Project Cash Flow

	Mar-11	Apr-11	May-11	Jun-11	Jul-11	Aug-11	Sep-11	Oct-11	Nov-11	Dec-11	Jan-12	Feb-12
Process	$250,000	$250,000	$250,000	$250,000	$250,000	$250,000						
Reengineering												
Supply Chain Tool						$100,000	$400,000	$125,000	$125,000	$125,000	$125,000	$125,000
Employee Time							$75,000	$75,000	$75,000	$75,000	$75,000	
Total Payment (Debt)	$250,000	$250,000	$250,000	$250,000	$250,000	$350,000	$600,000	$200,000	$200,000	$200,000	$200,000	$125,000

EXHIBIT 3.5 Marvelous Food's Proposed Project Outcome

Average Inventory	$1,724,644
Average Accounts Receivable	$555,289
Inventory Turnover Ratio	1.7
Days of Inventory on Hand	212.3
Accounts Receivable Collection Period	42
Return on Capital	14%
Return on Equity	23.84%

of the reductions in both of these ratios will have the same effect as a cash inflow, as the resulting reductions increase the availability of cash that Marvelous Food can use for other purposes. In this case, a part of the increased cash flow will be used to pay down the debt incurred by the project and to increase cash reserves, which were quite low.

That is good news, as is the effect of the project on Marvelous Food's financial ratios. Exhibit 3.5 presents the results that the proposed project could create if the goals are met. The exhibit presumes that in the first year of the project, Marvelous Food will be able to reduce the size of its inventory and accounts receivable by 50 percent each. The reductions, if they can be achieved, will reduce days of inventory on hand to 212.

The accounts receivable collection period will be reduced to 42 days. Return on capital will rise to 14 percent and return on equity to 23.84 percent, both of which are competitive in their industry. What is most interesting is that inventory turnover will rise to 1.7, still well below the industry average. If Marvelous Food can make other improvements that will complement the smaller inventory, it may be able to achieve results that could make the company an industry leader.

The goals illustrated in Exhibit 3.5 may be overly optimistic, but even if Marvelous Food can achieve only half of these results the first year with similar results in the second year followed by three to four years of incremental improvements, the project will have a profound impact on the company's financial picture.

We would normally consider this scenario at least twice: once based on WACC and once based on debt. We do this because the effect of debt is different from the effect of using WACC. When using WACC, the cost of the project incurs only an opportunity cost; in other words, the working capital that is used to improve the supply chain may not be used for other opportunities. In the case of using debt financing, there is another effect. When Marvelous Food incurs debt to complete the project, it also changes its leverage ratio (the weight of debt as compared to equity). One caveat to a small business: Using an average comparable WACC from similar companies can be misleading. A small company will normally pay a premium on new debt or outside capital investment due to higher risk for the lender or investor.

When projecting the ratios over time, we should see greater effects of the new cash flows in the short term. During the long term, we may not see as large a change in days of inventory on hand, but we may still see some incremental improvements. We will see the effect of the change in inventory days on the increased revenue that is projected over that time period, meaning that there may still be improvements beyond the time period when the cost of the project is reimbursed.

In the financial results that underlay the ratio calculation, we have assumed that the company will increase sales year over year at the industry average. Therefore, when we look at the figures, we must also consider whether this will occur. At present, when we compare Marvelous Food's ratios after the project to those before the project, we can see that the project will have a very positive effect on the company.

When project managers can perform such financial calculations, they will be able to help a company see the potential results of a project. In addition, project managers may also be able to help the company do risk analysis. For example, supposing that risk analysis showed that there was a very real potential for the project to be delayed by 9 to 12 months if internal resources needed to complete the analysis of the internal business processes were underestimated. Project managers can calculate what effect the additional time and cost would have on the project and therefore on the company financials.

STO Solution Model

In Chapter 1, we mentioned that according to the strategic, tactical, and operational (STO) model, problems often occurred when walls exist in the communications between different levels of a company. If we consider the Marvelous Food scenario, we could say that the supply chain project there is crucial to the company's ongoing success. In order to enhance the chances of success, all members of the project team must understand how their role is crucial to success and to company finances.

So, for example, when working with the internal resources of Marvelous Food to plan for business process engineering, the project manager can make the case by explaining the company's finances to the team and then showing how their efforts (or lack of them) will affect project cost and the company's financial results.

Of course, understanding how the project affects the company finances will be even greater if those financial results have a direct impact on employee income, such as salary increases or bonuses. If many of the employees hold company stock, they will certainly see the wisdom of improving company finances.

Now that we have examined a company's finances in order to understand how the project manager can judge projects based on those finances, we turn to how a company can put in place decision processes to ensure that all projects are judged by their effect on company financials. Here we examine the STO solution model and describe the process for implementing the model in a company.

The STO solution model presents a solution to the problem originally posed by the STO model. It contains the components necessary to create a strategy from a company's mission and objectives and to implement the strategy by carrying out the concrete steps necessary to make the strategy a reality. The model is a phased approach enabling a company to implement strategy across all levels. The model contains components that are implemented at the strategic, tactical, and operational levels of the company. We will review the components at a high level and then give a detailed description of how the components are implemented at a company. The next section is based on the STO model developed by the authors, as well as other materials.

The strategic components are meant to assist a company's executives to begin the process of linking mission and objectives to strategy. The process begins by assisting the executives of a company to review strategy and objectives with the goal of helping them, first of all, understand the difference between mission, objectives, and strategy. Not only do executives often misunderstand the meaning of each term, but also often they do not agree on what the company's mission and strategy are.

The company's financial objectives are an important part of these discussions. The mission and objectives orient the company's direction, but finance drives the strategy. Without appropriate financial direction, no company can survive for very long. Once the company has achieved clarity on its mission and objectives, it must set the strategy, that is, the concrete actions that must be taken in order to achieve the mission and objectives.

The company must then link the strategic and tactical by encouraging executives and senior and line management to transform strategy into a list of characteristics and other information to prioritize the firm's project portfolio. The project portfolio must be based on the strategy that the group has already laid out. Group members must also review resource utilization to further prioritize the project portfolio. Finally, they must create a sustaining process for ongoing project operations, which is known as portfolio management.

Implementing Strategy throughout the Company

The rest of this chapter explains the process of implementing a plan of strategy throughout a company. We cover these steps:

- Define the company mission.
- Set concrete objectives that move the mission forward.
- Develop the deliverables that accomplish the objectives.
- Create criteria for prioritizing objectives based on alignment with the mission, financial opportunity, and resource availability.
- Develop and prioritize the projects corresponding to the deliverables.
- Begin execution of the projects.
- Create a process to monitor results and prioritize and select future projects.

Business Action Framework

In addition to drawing on the STO solution model, we also draw on work by noted author and speaker Michael Hugos, who developed the theory and process that he named the Business Action Framework. The STO model points out that strategy, developed based on the mission and objectives of a company, must be driven down into the organization via portfolio management. The Business Action Framework provides a method of defining the mission, objectives, and strategy of a company.

The Business Action Framework employs the insights of the company's executives to determine any action that must be taken to advance the company success. Hugos points out that the action may be a response to a challenge or problem, or an attempt to capitalize on market conditions or to diversify the company's business activities. The framework is meant to bring the executives together in a forum that will provide the energy to move quickly. This is in line with the author's insistence in his recent book, *The Real Time Enterprise*, that in order to create significant change in a company, you must create a sense of urgency.[2]

After the company executives have identified the business context, they then must define the mission and critical objectives of the organization. As we have defined it in the STO solution model, the mission is a short statement that gives direction to the organization. The key to a mission is that it is long term. Companies do not change their missions every two or three years. In addition, the mission is a short statement, no more than three or four sentences, according to Hugos. Critical objectives, however, are "specific and measurable actions [that] must be taken in order to accomplish the Mission."[3] Critical objectives define the concrete steps that must be taken in order to accomplish the mission. In the STO solution model, strategy is the equivalent of critical objectives.

An essential step in the Business Action Framework is to map the critical objectives to the company's business functions, identifying the impact of each business function. The impact is evaluated based on how well each business function performs. In particular, poor performance in any function is highlighted. The areas of poor performance will become the focus of improvements that the company must make. In some cases, there may be no business process corresponding to the objective, pointing out the necessity of new development within the company.

Once the critical objectives have been mapped to business functions, the functions are sorted into a prioritized list based on how many objectives are impacted by the function and how well each function performs. Hugos defines those areas where objectives are impacted the most and are also most in need of improvement leverage points. The final step in the process is to study each leverage point in order to determine a course of action that will improve it. In essence, the group determines the projects that need to be performed in order to achieve the critical objectives and support the mission of the company.

An example of a company that used the Business Action Framework within the context of the STO solution model is a service company that does research and offers technical assistance to other companies. The company was in the process of transforming itself from being predominantly a research facility to becoming a more active consultant. Already well known for first-class research, the company wished to become more actively engaged in working with their clients to make improvements.

Company executives realized that they would also need to realign their operations in order to pursue their mission. Using the Business Action Framework in the context of a strategy review workshop, the group defined specific objectives that the company needed to achieve in order to be successful at its new mission. The objectives that they developed were:

- Increase business with current clients by offering assistance in addition to research
- Diversify by seeking new clients who would be interested in the consulting services
- Diversify geographically
- Better utilize resources by becoming more efficient and effective

The executive group then studied the company's business functions and determined what work was needed in different areas in order to be successful (for example, project management, project selection, and resource allocation). In addition to studying the situation as a group, each member of the executive team led a study by their own area of the firm to determine how well that area supported the objectives and what actions they would take in the upcoming year in order to support critical objectives.

By doing so, the company drove an understanding of the critical objectives all the way to the operational level of the company, and developed strategy at that level. The result was a much better alignment between what the company wished to achieve and the work that was taking place within the company.

Business Agility

Once a company has the processes in place to drive their strategy to the lowest level of the organization, they must have a way to acknowledge and react to changes in the business environment that can change strategy. In addition to defining the Business Action Framework, Michael Hugos has done groundbreaking work on Business Agility.[4]

The truly agile business is ready to respond quickly to whatever circumstances the economy throws at them. Hugos avers that if a business has the three basic systems of business agility: (1) Awareness, (2) Balance, and (3) Agility, that business will be able to focus and respond successfully to whatever the marketplace brings forth.

According to Hugos, there are three basic systems that form "loops" within a business that are the basis for agile operations. As mentioned above, those loops are Awareness, Balance, and Agility. The important concept here is that the three loops are interconnected, each one providing feedback to the other loops, without which the system would not work.

1. Awareness—The first loop places a strategic focus on the marketplace right now, gathering information about what is happening with customers, clients, and the marketplace in general. The information in the Awareness loop may come from outward looking systems, such as market research. However, inputs can be found in business systems such as ERP and CRM. Data mining or Business Intelligence software can also be helpful.
2. Balance—Information gathered by the Awareness loop becomes input for the Balance loop, which has two purposes. First, the balance loop reviews all processes to standardize as much as possible. In particular, business agility relies on standard processes that

can be automated to as great a degree as possible, allowing energy to be focused on the non-standard.

The second purpose of the Balance loop is to identify inputs from the Awareness loop that are non-standard. Any input that does not fit into an existing process is considered non-standard. The non-standard is what represents opportunity for the agile business.

3. Agility—The third loop receives input from the Balance loop and performs analysis to understand emerging opportunities and threats. In particular, the Balance loop plays a key role in the on-going implementation of strategy. When an opportunity or threat is identified, strategy guides the Agility loop in which concerns to actively address, and what new processes to put in place to take advantage of the new information.

In addition, the Balance loop also plays a crucial role in the on-going, incremental revision of strategy to meet the challenges that emerge. Strategy should not be a "once a year" activity. A vibrant, successful strategy must be transformed constantly if the business is to remain truly agile.

Portfolio Management

To ensure that strategy is actually being carried out in a company, the final link is portfolio management. In the Marvelous Food case, the project manager understood the financial information necessary to study the project's financial returns and the effect of those returns on Marvelous Food's financial performance. The project manager studied the returns of the supply chain project, as well as the financial implications of using debt or equity to finance the project and the implications of risk and schedule for company profitability.

The system that allows the project managers to have the information to make these determinations is project portfolio management.

EXHIBIT 3.6 Project Portfolio Management

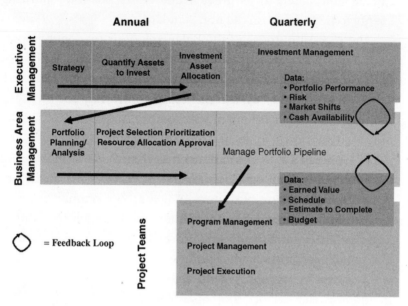

Project portfolio management is the process that links mission and objectives and strategy to the performance of individual project teams. In terms of the three levels in the STO solution model, strategic, tactical, and operational, project portfolio management is the tactical level, where decisions are made about what projects to carry out in support of the company's mission, objectives, and strategy.

In Exhibit 3.6, we see a graphic illustration of project portfolio management. In the upper or strategic level, executive management has devised a strategy based on the mission and objectives. That strategy, in addition to being based on mission and objectives, also was determined by decisions that executive management made on how to invest company assets.

For example, in the case of Marvelous Food, executive management decided to spend resources (people and money) on a new supply chain system that would reduce days of inventory on hand and improve cash flow. Let us say that they also decided to reengineer business processes in order to be more efficient about billing and collecting, so as to reduce receivable days. Management now has a strategy on how to use company resources in order to improve its finances.

Next, business area management will use project portfolio management to select projects based on the priorities that the executives had determined. In this case, they considered both the supply chain project and the business process reengineering project for billing and receivables. Other projects and activities also are planned for the year, but supply chain and business process reengineering have the highest priority.

The project portfolio management group selects projects and allocates resources based on how much work can be done. This is sometimes referred to as determining the size of the pipeline. The group looks at resources available and then decides what projects can be done with the resources at hand.

In the Marvelous Food case, the area managers determined that a significant number of resources would be needed for both the supply chain project and the business reengineering project for billing and receivables. The supply chain project would also require business process reengineering prior to the deployment of the actual application. As a result, the managers decided to time the business process reengineering process to begin when the first phase of the supply chain project was complete.

Besides determining the size of the pipeline of projects to be performed, the project portfolio management group has one other crucial task: collecting information and providing feedback to executive management, or "maintaining the pipeline." In doing so, the portfolio management group must use two sets of objectives to determine how well the company is performing: project objectives and business objectives.

Regarding project objectives, the group asks: Are projects performing on time, on budget, and within scope? Are there any problems or risks that are endangering the projects? Is quality at acceptable levels?

Regarding business objectives, the group asks: Is there anything in the business landscape that has changed? Is the company still pursuing the right mix of projects?

Both sets of objectives imply that the portfolio management group is maintaining feedback between the different levels of the company. As we can see in Exhibit 3.6, the group maintains constant feedback among the three levels of the company.

If problems occur in the various projects that the firm is carrying out, or if market conditions change, the portfolio management group is positioned to react quickly and make changes. If, for example, executives discover that sales of a particular food project are slipping and through market research learn that a competitor has introduced a new product into the marketplace, they can then alert the portfolio management group that something must be done to counter the competition.

The group can review the status of current projects and resources, and react. In this case, group members may decide to shift cash resources away from the business process reengineering of billing and receivables and invest in product development to counter the competition.

It has become fashionable in business to talk about pushing business decision making "out" into the organization; in other words, the executive determines the what, but the management situated close to the action decides the how. The portfolio management group, when it is comprised of the right mix of staff and line management, is able to perform the how with dexterity and speed.

Conclusion

It is clear from our study of the effect of a company's financial goals and performance that a company's strategy must be oriented by mission and objectives, but strategy must be driven by finances. In other words, finance represents the engine that allows a company to move forward and accomplish its mission and objectives. It is also clear that strategy must be made up of the concrete steps that the company must take in order to be successful.

Project managers must learn as much as possible about the company's mission, objectives, and strategy to be able to determine whether a particular project meets the company's strategic financial objectives. Using the financial ratios of the DuPont Method, we have shown how project managers can decide if a project will be viable; in other words, will it provide cash inflow that is worth more than the cash outflow? Will it be more efficient to finance the project with cash from equity or by increasing debt? Will the results of the project have a positive effect on overall financial performance?

We have also shown how project managers can assist a company in determining what its mission and objectives are and what concrete steps the company must take in order to create a strategy to reach the mission and objectives. The Business Action Framework is a step-by-step method for implementing strategy.

Finally, we have shown how proper management of both resources and money according to priorities set by the mission, objectives, and strategy can be central to keeping the company working on an even keel and able to respond quickly and effectively to changes in internal or external circumstances.

Notes

1. For more information on the project charter and other project tools, see our previous book: Kevin Callahan, Lynne Brooks, *The Essentials of Strategic Project Management* (Hoboken, NJ: John Wiley & Sons, 2004).

2. Michael H. Hugos, *The Real Time Enterprise* (Hoboken, NJ: John Wiley & Sons, 2005).

3. Michael H. Hugos, The Business Action Framework, (c) 2006 Michael H. Hugos.

4. Ibid.

CHAPTER 4

Cost

When considering the topic of cost, a project manager may well ask, "Doesn't the project budget cover cost?" The answer is . . . it depends! Budget, first of all, is concerned with three areas: predicting what income and expenses will be, monitoring expenses and cash flow, and producing information to predict profit and loss. Cost, however, is concerned with analyzing the source and behavior of cost, its effect on finances, and the processes used to manage cost in an optimal way.

To further illustrate the difference between budget and cost, let's look at two examples. It will become clear why we differentiate between the two.

Let's take a new product development project as an example. The project will develop a new widget, and the budget contains the information shown in Exhibit 4.1.

EXHIBIT 4.1 Widget Budget

Cost	Amount
Direct Labor	$20,000
Materials	$5,000
Machinery—Setup for Four Widgets	$1,000 × 4 = $4,000
Machinery—Use Four Hours for Four Widgets	$250 × 4 = $1,000 × 4 = $4,000
Machinery—Total	$10,000

There are three components to the cost of the project: labor, materials, and machinery. (We will ignore overhead for the moment.) The materials and machinery will be used to create prototypes, and the cost of each prototype is $3,000. It seems like we have all the information to move ahead.

However, a closer look at how the costs of this project behave may reveal useful information to the astute project manager. The machinery cost actually contains two components: a setup cost of $1,000 and an hourly usage rate of $250. The budget assumes that each prototype will take four hours to create. Every time that the machine is set up to produce a prototype, there is a charge of $1,000. Assuming that it takes four hours to produce a prototype, the cost of using the machine is also $1,000. This is an example of what is called a semi-variable cost; part of the cost is fixed (the setup) and part of the cost is variable (producing the prototype), depending on the time the machine is used.

Knowing that there is a semi-variable cost can be useful in doing a risk analysis. For example, suppose that problems in creating several of the prototypes made it necessary to produce seven prototypes instead of five; what would the total cost of prototypes then be: $21,000? $15,000? If, for example, the first prototype was spoiled after only an hour, it would have cost $1,250 instead of $2,000, as three hours of machine time were not used. However, there would be an additional $1,000 setup cost to replace the first prototype. Knowledge of how this cost behaves would certainly help in the risk analysis of this project.

Let's look at another example of how cost analysis can assist project managers in a service project. ABC is a small company that specializes in business process engineering. Good cost management is vital to maintaining a profitable enterprise. ABC Company does not keep a lot of resources on the bench, so partners and employees are expected to perform contract work and seek out new work.

While it is relatively easy for ABC Company to track costs related directly to any particular project, it is more difficult to quantify non-billable hours that are spent negotiating a particular contract with a client. Generally, sales and marketing activities are indirect expenses not linked to a particular client. However, in some cases, where the contract negotiation requires specific additional work to be done, it may be necessary to track that work and attribute the cost to the client.

For example, if ABC were going to produce a single customized piece of equipment for a client, it may be necessary to incur specific engineering costs in order to verify that the company can actually produce the equipment. If the costs are incurred before a contract is signed, ABC must have a way of capturing those costs and including them in the project's overhead.

As we can see from the examples, different cost techniques allow companies to properly understand the source and type of cost and to use processes that allow them to recover the costs in order to maintain a profitable enterprise. Project managers who wish to improve the performance of their projects will benefit from a better understanding of how cost is handled in their organization.

It is important to remember that cost may be quite different as it applies to projects, compared to operations. Projects are unique endeavors with a beginning and end that produce a deliverable. Operations, however, are the ongoing business processes that produce goods and services in a repetitive manner. Producing cars in a factory is operations; creating the prototype of a new car is a project. As we explore the different facets of cost, we will also look at how that knowledge can be useful to project managers. In this chapter, we introduce the basics of cost and help project managers better understand how those basics may relate to their projects.

Definition and Purpose of Cost

Cost is the measurement of resources that must be expended in order to obtain an object or complete an activity. Cost is usually expressed in monetary terms, as in employee time; the materials to manufacture an object may be represented by their monetary value.

Cost normally falls into the domain of managerial accounting and has four essential purposes.

1. It is used for planning for future activities or budgets.
2. It is used for decision making throughout an organization.
3. It is used to compare actual results with budgets and determine why there are variances.
4. It is used to calculate income from the company's operations and projects.

The nature and form of cost can vary across organizations. In the United States, there are three basic types of organizations: manufacturing, retail, and service. Although manufacturing once was the greatest portion of the U.S. economy, the retail sector is also significant, and the service sector now actually makes up the largest portion of the economy.

Cost Classifications

Costs are classified according to the purpose of the cost information that is sought (see Exhibit 4.2). Product and period costs provide information needed to create external financial statements, such as the income statement and balance sheet. Cost behavior helps a company look into the future by seeing how costs may change based on other changing variables, such as demand or production rate, or how a fixed cost affects different situations. Costs must also be assigned to a source, giving rise to the concept of direct and indirect costs.

At other times, cost information supports business decisions, such as understanding the differential between costs of two possibilities or the cost of pursuing one opportunity over another. Finally, cost of quality compares the cost of preventing defects as opposed to correcting defects and the cost of providing a warranty on products or services.

The rest of this chapter explains each cost classification and describes its importance to project management.

EXHIBIT 4.2 Cost Classifications*

Financial Statements	Cost Decisions
■ Product Cost	■ Differential Costs
■ Period Cost	■ Sunk Costs
	■ Opportunity Costs
Cost Behavior	
■ Variable	**Cost of Quality**
■ Fixed	■ Prevention
■ Semi-variable	■ Correction
	■ Warranty
Assigning Costs	
■ Direct	
■ Indirect	

*Based on an illustration from Ray Garrison & Eric Noreen, *Managerial Accounting* (New York: McGraw-Hill, 2003).

Product and Period Cost

Period and product costs provide information to create financial statements for external use. In order to better explain these costs, we need to return briefly to some basic concepts of cost accounting. As you will recall from Chapter 2, the matching principle of accrual accounting holds that cost is recognized at the time when the benefit that the cost provides occurs. For example, if a company pays for liability insurance for two years in advance, the cost of insuring the company for this year only will be reflected or accrued to this year's income and expense statement. In other words, the company derives only part of the benefit of the insurance premium this year, so it can claim only that part of the premium as an expense this year.

However, the cost to acquire or make a product to sell or provide a service is recognized when the sale of the product or service triggers revenue. For example, a company that manufactures toys will recognize the cost of manufacturing that toy in the same time period when that toy is sold. If the toy is not sold during the same time period when it is made, then the cost of making the toy is held over, or accrued to the time period when it is sold.

With this accrual principle in mind, let's look at product cost. Product cost is the sum of all costs that are directly linked to the production or acquisition of a product or service to be sold later. Product costs might include direct materials and direct labor for a product, programming time for a piece of software, or professional time for creating a new service—such as training—to be sold. The cost of marketing and selling that product or service is not included in the product cost because they can be very difficult to link directly to the product or service.

Period costs are all costs that are not related directly to creating the product or service and may fall into several categories. For example, the cost of administration of a company or for marketing and sales cannot be directly linked to the production of an individual product. In addition, the cost of administration, such as human resources services, salaries, or insurance and rent cannot be linked directly to a product or service. These are period costs that are recognized as expenses when the benefit occurs. For some, the benefit is immediate; for others (such as the insurance example) the benefit is recognized later.

It is important for project managers to recognize the difference between when the cost is recognized for accounting purposes and when it actually occurs. Although the cost of programming time may be recognized only when the software is sold, the actual expense occurs during project execution. This means that cash flow out of the company occurs before the expense that causes the cash outflow is recognized and that outflow has a real effect on the company bank account. Refer to Chapter 6 for more information on cash flow.

Cost Behavior

Cost behavior is valuable in predicting future cost when creating budgets or planning for future activities such as production or projects.

Certain activities affect cost in different ways. In the manufacturing example discussed earlier, we discovered that the fixed setup cost and variable machine time cost of making prototypes could yield costs that were quite different from what was originally expected.

If there were problems with the machining process early on and additional prototypes had to be made, costs would go up quickly due to the $1,000 fixed price of the machine setup, no matter how many hours the machine was used to create an individual prototype. Advance knowledge of the cost structure can lead to greater care in planning the process so as to avoid waste and increased cost.

There are three major types of cost behavior: (1) variable, (2) fixed, and (3) semi-variable. However, often there are more subtle nuances to how each cost behavior will react in a given situation.

VARIABLE COSTS   Variable costs are those that change in direct relationship to changes in the activity that triggers the cost. For example, the cost of the material needed to manufacture a bolt increases in direct proportion to the number of bolts that are manufactured. A grocery retailer will incur increased cost as more containers of milk are sold. A consulting company will incur increased cost for each hour of service provided by hourly consultants.

In essence, a variable cost is a fixed amount of cost per unit produced or activity used. As the units produced or activities increase, the cost increases by the same proportion. If more bolts are produced, the cost will increase by the same amount for each bolt. If more milk is sold, the cost will increase by the same amount for each container; and if more consulting hours are delivered, the cost increases by the same amount for each hour of service.

There are other costs that, although variable, can be obtained only in large quantities. For example, retailers may have to buy suits by lots of 100. It is possible that the more lots they buy, the cheaper the overall price. A single lot of 100 might be $7,000, or $70 a suit. Five lots of suits, however, might be $25,000, or $50 a suit.

The more they buy, the less cost per unit. This type of cost is called step variable.

For another example, consider a service company that provides consulting to its clients at an hourly rate. The company pays employees a salary and no overtime. Calculating the real cost of resources can become tricky under certain circumstances, yet it is crucial to understand the real costs in order to predict and identify profitability.

Let us take a single employee of the company who is working 50 percent on a client project, 80 hours a month. The employee's hourly rate is the salary for the month plus benefits divided by 160. This seems to be a variable rate; the more the employee works for the client, the more cost is charged to the project.

However, what if the employee, who also bills 80 hours a month to another project, should work 20 hours overtime to the project? The employee has now worked 180 hours in the month, but the actual overall cost has not changed because he is paid a salary. The new calculation would be salary plus benefits divided by 180, lowering the overall hourly cost for that resource. If the project manager calculates the cost of the employee in the normal manner, then the project is being overcharged for the cost of the resource. In this case, we can say that the employee's rate is variable within the relevant range. In this case the relevant range is 160 hours.

Of course, the delicate balance for the company is between the number of hours over 160 it can have employees work, thereby boosting profitability, and the point where employees become frustrated with unpaid overtime.

FIXED COSTS In contrast to variable costs, fixed costs remain the same despite increases or decreases in business activity. For example, a manufacturing plant must heat the plant during the winter whether production increases or decreases. The grocery retailer that rents its building must pay the rent no matter how many containers of milk are sold, and the service company must pay the rent for its offices, whether billable hours increase or decrease.

Fixed costs have characteristics that are different from variable costs. For example, while the cost of heating cannot be directly related to the bolts produced at the factory, the cost of heating must be included in the bolt's cost. Therefore, fixed costs actually react in the opposite way to variable costs; if the plant produced 100,000 bolts this month, and heating cost was $2,000, then each bolt would have to include $0.02 cost of heating.

Although the fixed cost does not rise or fall in response to the activity, in this case, manufacturing bolts, the effect on the cost of producing the bolts does respond to the level of activity. Should production of the bolts decline by 50 percent, then the cost of heating on each bolt would rise to $0.04.

In addition, fixed costs may or may not be controllable. It is up to management to decide whether to use those resources and incur the cost. If incurred, the cost would be fixed.

Committed fixed costs cannot be controlled. The example of heat in the plant manufacturing bolts is non-discretionary. A service company may subcontract consultants for a fixed fee per month, but a cancellation clause in the contract would be an example of non-committed or discretionary fixed cost.

SEMI-VARIABLE COSTS   Semi-variable costs contain both fixed and variable elements. The real key is in being able to identify each element of semi-variable costs. In the new product development project example, the project budget predicts that the overall cost of producing a prototype is $3,000. However, we discovered that the cost could be broken down into three major components: materials, direct labor, and machine costs.

On closer observation, we realized that the machine cost had two elements as well: setup costs, which did not change from one prototype to the next, and machine hours, which could change. What drives the fixed portion of the cost is that machine setup costs are the same regardless of how many hours it took to create the prototype.

Assigning Costs

DIRECT COSTS Based on our initial definition of cost, a direct cost is the measure of resources that must be given in order to obtain an object or complete an activity that can be directly related to that object or activity. In a manufacturing setting, direct materials and labor would be direct costs. In a retail industry, the cost of acquiring goods for sale would be a direct cost. In a service industry, the cost of paying the employee to do consulting is a direct cost.

INDIRECT COSTS Indirect costs are those costs that are not related directly to the object or activity that produce a project or service. Referring to previous examples, the cost of heating a factory is an indirect cost, as are the salaries of administrators not directly working on the production of goods or services.

Cost Decisions

Project managers are often called on to make decisions between different opportunities or different ways of accomplishing the goals and objectives of a company. The three types of cost that are used to make decisions are differential cost, sunk cost, and opportunity cost.

Differential Cost

Differential cost is simply the difference in cost between choosing one of two or more options to pursue. The other side of differential cost is differential revenue. When considering the different options to pursue, the differential cost and revenue of each option is reviewed, and the option that presents the higher income usually is chosen.

Let's look at an example of how differential cost may be used to choose between two options. ABC Web Company creates and supports Internet web sites for other companies. Often its revenues are tied, in part, to the success of the web sites it designs. ABC Web has

EXHIBIT 4.3 Differential Costs

	In House Production	Sub-Contracted	Differential Revenues
Revenues from Site Production	$ 50,000	$ 50,000	$ 0
Commissions (Monthly)*	$ 90,000	$120,000	$30,000
Cost of Production	($35,000)	($45,000)	−$10,000
Gross Profit	$105,000	$125,000	$20,000
Overhead	($2,000)	($2,000)	$ 0
Net Revenue	$103,000	$123,000	$20,000

*Project Monthly Commission $10,000

been approached to produce a web site that it feels will be very successful, but currently its resources are working over capacity and cannot begin the work immediately.

ABC Web's alternatives are to ask the client to wait three months or to subcontract the work to another vendor that it has worked with in the past. The client has indicated that if ABC waits three months, it will pay a commission on the site's revenues for only 9 months instead of 12. Yet subcontracting is fairly expensive. Here is the differential calculation that ABC Web made:

According to this analysis, the differential revenues were $30,000, while the differential costs were $10,000, meaning that ABC Web would have $10,000 more revenue by choosing to subcontract this project to a vendor. By doing a differential cost study such as this, ABC Web is able to make a decision (see Exhibit 4.3).

SUNK COSTS   A sunk cost is any cost that is already incurred or sunk into a project. At times, when making decisions, managers may not wish to throw away money that has already been spent and will decide to continue so as to recoup the money already spent. This happens frequently in projects that are not going well. For example, take a software development project that was budgeted to cost $300,000.

Now, with the delivery date six months past and the cost topping $400,000, the company must make a decision as to whether to continue or not.

Several of the programmers on the project want to continue. They say, "We think we are almost there, and besides, we've already spent $400,000. We don't want to waste the money!" However, the money that has been spent is gone (or sunk). It must not enter into the decision. The decision as to whether to continue or not should be made only on the chances of successfully completing the project, no matter what costs have already been sunk into it.

Therefore, spending more money when the success of the project is not clear (or when failure is all too clear) is not justified. In reality, since the money is already spent, it cannot be used to make future decisions. Sunk costs should never have a place in deciding future activities or operations.

OPPORTUNITY COSTS   Opportunity cost results when a decision is made to pursue one benefit over another. Although opportunity cost is important in making decisions, it is not a cost that enters into accounting statements, such as income expense reports or balance sheets. Some examples of opportunity cost could be:

- The selection of one project over another. Since both projects represent potential revenue to the company, the revenue of the project not chosen is an opportunity cost.
- Not pursuing a particular new product in order to invest in other areas. The potential revenue of this product is an opportunity cost.

As we can see in each of the decision costs descriptions, often the information used to make a decision comes from the same source and is in a similar format as other costs, but is used for a different purpose. For example, in the differential cost example the production cost of the software could include variable, semi-variable, and fixed cost, but in order to make a decision about whether to subcontract, the type of cost was less important than the difference in cost between the two options.

Cost of Quality

An old adage about quality goes, "You can't inspect in quality." In other words, no matter how much you inspect a product or a service, if you are not putting quality into the work being done, you can't inspect it in after the fact. You will wind up spending a lot of money either correcting the problem immediately or correcting it later. The longer you wait to correct, the more expensive the correction.

We define quality as fitness for use according to the original design of the product or service. As we said in *The Essentials of Strategic Project Management*, quality is the answer to "the two simple questions: 'What is it?' and 'What does it do?'"

The first criterion of quality is whether the product or service is what it is supposed to be. During quality planning, you must take up the answer to this question and decide how you would know if the end deliverable is what it is supposed to be. On a technical project, this might involve a comparison with the detailed specification of a product or software. On a non-technical project—for example, a project to reengineer a business process, this would be a comparison with the proposed workflow of the new process.

The three costs associated with quality are prevention costs, correction costs, and warranty costs. As indicated, quality costs are a balance between preventing mistakes and discovering and correcting them.

Prevention

The best place to ensure quality in a product or service is at the time that the product or service is created. The cost of prevention includes all of the activities that take place to ensure that the product or service can meet the standard established by the two questions, what is it and what does it do. In the case of a new product, this may be engineering tests; for a service, it may be a pilot test.

When planning for the execution of a project, be sure that the cost of preventing mistakes and ensuring quality does not become more expensive than the price the product or service can bear in a competitive marketplace or more than can be charged for the product or service.

Correction

The cost of correction includes all of the activities that take place to find and correct problems. Correcting problems can be a costly enterprise. Several years ago, Porsche, the celebrated car maker, experienced problems in sustaining profitability. It was becoming too costly to produce the cars. Research uncovered an actual "culture of correction" that was inhibiting Porsche's fortunes.

Porsche's manufacturing processes were actually not up to par, but in the Porsche culture, engineers were proud of their ability to find and solve problems in individual automobiles. When a car came off of the assembly line and inspection showed multiple problems, engineers prided themselves on being able to fix them, but at what cost?

Porsche had to undergo a cultural shift that gradually shifted the engineers' pride from being able to correct problems to being able to engineer and manufacture cars without the problems.

Warranty

The cost of warranty includes all of those activities that correct problems that occur after the product or service has been sold. Normally, this is the most expensive quality cost. It can involve return, repair, or replacement of merchandise and rework of services. Although warranty expenses may seem obvious in the manufacturing and retail industries, poor programming and the resulting debugging often can take a great deal of time and be very expensive.

For smaller, less expensive goods, however, it is often cheaper for manufacturers simply to replace the item and throw away the bad one. These days, most people would not even try to repair a less expensive DVD or CD player. If the player was under warranty, they would receive a new one. If it was not, they would simply throw it away and buy a new one.

Cost and Industry

Now let's take a look at how cost affects the finances of companies in the different industry categories: service, merchandising, and manufacturing. Exhibit 4.4 illustrates a simplified income and expense statement for fictitious companies in each industry. The statement is somewhat simplified, containing only those expenses that directly relate to operating a company and giving net operating profit (what is left before the company pays taxes, interest on debt, and accounts for depreciation and amortization; also known as EBITDA).

Service Industry

At first glance, it seems like the service industry has the simpler situation. All of the expenses are categorized as direct client expenses and are presumably period costs that are expensed in the period in which they are incurred. This would certainly be true of any service company that does consulting for a fee. However, when we explore the range of service companies, it becomes apparent that it is not that simple.

An example of a service company might be an actuarial firm that provides advice to clients on retirement programs. The company is paid a fee for the services and in turn pays its consultants for performing the work. Let's suppose that a client contracts the actuarial company to create a piece of software that provides the same advice in a

EXHIBIT 4.4 Cost and Industry[*]

Income and Expense Statement December 31, 2010

	Service	Merchandising	Manufacturing
	Leman Consulting Group	Burkhouse Distributors	Warren Manufacturing
Sales	$ 10,000,000	$10,000,000	$10,000,000
Expenses			
Cost of Goods Manufactured			
Materials Purchased			$ 3,200,000
Beginning Materials Inventory			$ 875,000
Ending Materials Inventory			($649,000)
Total Materials Used			$ 3,426,000
Direct Labor			$ 1,200,000
Manufacturing Overhead			$ 1,450,000
Total Manufacturing Costs			$ 6,076,000
Beginning Work in Process			$ 325,000
Ending Work in Process			($310,000)
Cost of Goods Manufactured			$ 6,091,000
Purchases		$ 6,450,000	
Beginning Inventory Finished Goods		$ 1,820,000	$ 250,000
Ending Inventory Finished Goods		($1,955,000)	($225,000)
Cost of Goods Sold		$ 6,315,000	$ 6,116,000
Client Expenses	$ 7,650,000		
Gross Profits	$ 2,350,000	$ 3,685,000	$ 3,884,000
Operating Expenses			
Sales	$ 1,400,000	$ 1,700,000	$ 1,200,000
Administration	$ 225,000	$ 875,000	$ 1,150,000
Net Operating Income	$ 725,000	$ 1,110,000	$ 1,534,000

[*]Based on an illustration from Arnold Schneider and Harold M. Sollenberger, *Managerial Accounting Manufacturing and Service Applications*, Third Edition (Mason, Ohio: Thomson Custom Publishing, 2003).

fashion that makes it easier for the client to use. Whether the software is produced directly by the company or outsourced to a vendor, the costs are still direct client expenses and period costs.

However, if the company decides to develop that software for sale to the general market, the manner in which costs behave may change. The period cost may become a product cost, and the development activities must then be linked back to the product. As a result, the service company may have a cost structure that resembles that of a manufacturing company, but without any direct materials! The rise of research and development within the software industry has given birth to entire new areas of accounting guidelines and law.

Even in a more traditional service setting such as a hospital, costs may act more like those in a manufacturing company. For example, the cost of hip surgery for a patient might include direct labor costs, such as the surgeon's fees, and direct materials costs, including hip replacement hardware and various materials used. The surgery would also include direct overhead for the operating room and indirect overhead for general hospital infrastructure. An analysis of the operating room overhead may reveal both fixed costs (electricity) and variable costs (cleanup time after surgery).

The service industry also incurs operating expenses. As implied by the name, operating expenses are incurred in the everyday operations of the company. The distinction between operating expenses and the other types of expenses seen in the income and expense statement is that operating expenses cannot be attributed directly to the services that the company provides.

Therefore, operating expenses are considered period costs and expensed in the period in which they are incurred. A portion of operating expenses will most likely be fixed cost, such as the cost of running facilities or the cost of administrative staff. Others, such as sales costs, may be related variable costs, depending on the level of sales.

Thus, it is clear that looking at a simple income and expense statement may not reveal all the information that you need to know about a company in order to determine how costs affect it.

Retail Industry

The retail industry introduces a new element to our income and expense statement: cost of goods sold. This variable implies that there is a cost to what is being sold beyond the direct client costs that we saw in the service industry. Cost of goods sold has two subsets: cost of goods manufactured and cost of goods purchased. We will look only at the latter while discussing the merchandising industry.

Cost of goods purchased introduces inventory into the cost equation for a company. Whether the merchandising company is a wholesale distributor or a retail seller, it must have something on hand to sell. As we can see from the income and expense statement, Burkhouse Distributors had inventory on hand at the beginning of the year because inventory is a product cost and can be expensed only when the inventory in question is actually sold. Unsold inventory remains on the books until it is sold (or otherwise disposed of). If you were to look at Burkhouse Distributors' balance sheet, you would see that the beginning inventory is also listed as an asset.

In addition to being a product cost, inventory is a variable cost; the more inventory that is purchased, the higher the cost. However, at times inventory may be a step-variable cost. For example, if there is a volume discount, then the cost would vary, but only by the steps allowed in the volume discounts. Think of the suits we mentioned earlier in the chapter; 100 suits may cost $7,000 or $70 a suit, while 500 suits may cost $25,000 or $50 a suit. The purchaser can only benefit from decrease in cost at the "step" of 500 suits.

As with the service industry, the merchandising industry also has operating expenses. In addition to general selling and administration expenses, the merchandising industry may have other types of overhead costs, such as warehousing and transportation costs, which will be a mix of variable and fixed costs. Some costs associated with a warehouse will most likely be fixed, although recent rising fuel costs might not seem very "fixed." Trucking costs would be considered variable; the more goods that need to be moved, the higher the costs.

Manufacturing Industry

The manufacturing industry presents a more complex picture of cost. Most of that complexity is due to the introduction of the other subset of cost of goods: cost of manufacturing. Cost of manufacturing has a number of components that contribute to the final cost of an individual product:

- *Direct Material Cost.* The cost of purchasing the materials that are transformed into the final product.
- *Direct Labor Cost.* The cost of the people that perform the manufacturing process.
- *Work in Progress (WIP).* The cost of partially completed products at the end of an accounting period. Warren Manufacturing had a certain amount of unfinished goods in the pipeline at the end of 2010.
- *Indirect Cost of Manufacturing.* The overhead cost of manufacturing that can be directly attributed to the manufacturing process; for example, the maintenance cost of a machine that is used in the process can be attributed to the products that are manufactured with it.
- *Finished Goods Cost.* The total cost of producing units of the product.

The key to understanding cost and the manufacturing process is in the state of the material that is being transformed. During the manufacturing process, materials are transformed by labor to become finished goods. Often a product goes through more than one stage during the process. Work in process is any intermediary state between direct material and finished good.

WIP also implies that cost (value) has been added to a product along the way. Ken Milani,[1] professor of management at the University of Notre Dame, explains the concept with a fictitious salami manufacturing operation. First, meat must be chopped and then mixed with spices. Next it is formed into its shape, and finally it is packaged. At each step of the way, direct labor cost is added. In some stages, additional direct material cost is added as well. Therefore, WIP at the end of the mixing stage includes direct labor cost for chopping and mixing and direct materials cost for meat and spices.

Professor Milani also points out that at the end of the process certain indirect costs are added to the salami as well, such as the cost of cleaning and maintaining the machines that are used in the process.

All of the costs associated with the manufacturing process are product costs, which must be tracked in order to calculate the final cost of the product. Inventory keeps track of product costs before the product is sold. A good part of managerial accounting is given over to tracking costs through the intermediary stages of manufacturing, each of which has an inventory, until the finished goods are sold and the revenues and expenses are accounted for.

If we return to the income and expense statement for Warren Manufacturing, we see that the company has a finished goods inventory but has no figure in purchasing. Warren's inventory is made up of goods that have been manufactured by the company.

Conclusion

As we have seen, cost is a complex subject that reaches far beyond the individual budget of any given project. Different areas of the company use cost information in different ways, and the information must be formulated to suit the company area that it serves.

When project managers are planning a project, and in particular are creating a project budget, knowledge of the different kinds of costs that the project will incur is essential to successful budgeting. In addition, an understanding of overall cost at a particular company in a specific industry will help project managers create budgets that take cost into proper consideration and deliver winning results.

Note

1. Kenneth W. Milani, Ph. D., Mendoza College, University of Notre Dame, Notre Dame, Indiana.

CHAPTER 5

Project Financing

The objective of this chapter is to acquaint project managers with sources of funding for a given project, explain the implications of the costs associated with the source of funding, and describe the method for calculating the client's cost of funding. The focus is on funding at the macrolevel, or the effect on the company as a whole. Chapter 6 focuses on the costs of funding individual projects on the micro-level. Regardless of the level, there are two categories of sources for funding: debt (borrowing) and equity. It is important to note that the funding sources are also the sole providers of a company's assets.

Debt Financing

Borrowing

There are essentially four types of debt financing: (1) borrowing, (2) corporate bonds, (3) trade debt, and (4) customer deposits. The most common type of debt financing is borrowing from financial institutions, such as banks or leasing companies. Borrowing from financial institutions can be quick and relatively inexpensive.

Financial institutions borrow money at one rate and lend it out at a higher rate. The spread between the cost and the amount charged for the borrowing is how financial institutions make money. They do not set out trying to figure out how to make money on a defaulted loan. An organization that does plan to make money on a defaulted loan or places borrowers in a position where they can't retire their debt is known as a predatory lender.

Most financial institutions are regulated by licensing authorities, which have rules and regulations that prohibit predatory lending. It has been often argued that today's credit card companies do practice predatory lending, but there has been limited enforcement. Accordingly, the predominant business model is to expect orderly repayment of the loan.

To ensure payment of the loan, financial institutions consider what is referred to as the Four Cs of lending: credit, collateral, cash flow, and character. The credit component is concerned with the borrowing and repayment history of the borrower. Financial institutions like to see that the borrower has borrowed money in the past and has made timely payments. A history of borrowing and prompt payments indicates to lenders that the borrower takes his obligations seriously.

Collateral refers to assets that have been pledged as security in case of default on the loan. The collateral component is concerned with the value of the underlying assets that have been pledged and how easy those assets are to liquidate or turn to cash. The underlying theory here is that if something was worth $1 million and a borrower defaults on a $100,000 loan, the borrower would be motivated to liquidate the asset and preserve equity in that asset.

The cash flow component is concerned with the borrower's ability to make payments out of their normal income streams. In the industry this is referred to as DSCR (debt service coverage ratio) or TBCR (times burden covered ratio); these ratios were covered in Chapter 2. Typically the financial institution industry likes to see TBCRs greater than 1.25.

Finally, the character component deals with the borrower's reputation and perceived capabilities. Credit, collateral, and cash flow are all quantitatively measured. However, the character component is not. The criteria for establishing good or bad character vary from institution as well as case by case. Some of the more obvious negative criteria are felony convictions, frequent litigation, and inexperience. Be aware that the criteria for negative connotation may be much more subtle.

The Four Cs of lending are considered in aggregate. The inability to score well in all four will cause an increase in the rates that the borrower will pay. The underlying theory here is that the more risky the loan, the greater the return required (or higher the interest rate charged) by the lender.

Numerous types of borrowing products are available. Typically the lending product is tied to the life of the underlying assets.

Corporate Bonds

The second type of debt financing is corporate debt or bonds. A bond is a security sold to an investor. It is a contractual obligation between the issuer and the holder. The issuer promises to make interest payments to the holder at specific dates and to return the principal at a certain date (maturity). Bonds must be registered with the Securities and Exchange Commission (SEC). One other difference between a loan and a bond is that typically a loan is considered a claim on an asset and a bond is a claim on a specified stream of income.

The amount of the bond to be paid at maturity is called the bond's face value. The rate of interest to be paid by the issuer is called the coupon rate. You may wonder why the coupon rate is important. The answer lies in the fact that the duration of a bond is usually for a period of 10 to 30 years. Interest rates can vary with the market. If the coupon rate of a bond is 5 percent and the current interest rates are expected to be 10 percent, then that bond will sell at a discount.

When a bond is sold at a discount, it costs less than its face value. It would have to sell at less than its face value in order to compensate for the coupon rate of 5 percent versus a market of 10 percent. Be mindful that the issuer has to pay the face value at maturity. In the case where the coupon rate is 5 percent and the market is demanding

2 percent, the bond would trade for an amount greater than its face value. The amount over and above face value is called a bond premium.

Bonds also can have call provisions. The call provision allows the issuer to pay off the bonds at an earlier date if it can redeploy a new issue at lower coupon rates. There also is a feature referred to as a put bond, which allows the holder to extend the bond's maturity date in a declining interest rate environment or to require the issuer to retire the bond prior to maturity in a rising interest rate environment.

There are three additional types of corporate bonds: floating rate bonds, convertible bonds, and zero-coupon bonds. Floating rate bonds adjust their coupon rates to some sort of index, such as Treasury bill rates. They typically don't trade at premiums or discounts unless the issuer's financial strength changes. Convertible bonds allow the holders to exchange the bond for a set number of shares of stock.

Zero-coupon bonds, as the name implies, have a zero coupon rate. The bond sells for a calculated discount, the same as other bond discounts, and the holder receives no payments. At maturity the holder receives the bond's face value. The difference between what was paid and the face value effectively becomes the interest paid on the initial investment.

The time it takes to put together a bond offering, find an underwriter, and receive SEC approval can be significant. In addition, the underwriting fees can be staggering.

Trade Debt

Trade debt financing is a fancy phrase for extending accounts payable. The objective here is to delay payment of the payables beyond the sales and accounts receivable collection cycles. At first glance, this method of financing appears to be a cheap source of money. However, be aware of two concerns. Many vendors offer prompt-pay discounts, often between 1 percent and 3 percent of the bill.

Ignoring this discount can cost the client an additional 12 percent to 36 percent per year.

The second concern has to do with the impact on two of the Cs in lending, credit and character. As indicated earlier, a poor credit or character score will increase the cost on borrowed money.

Customer Deposits (Retainers)

Customer deposits (retainers) are similar in concept to financing the project with trade debt. The difference is that instead of extending trade debt, the project is financed through customer deposits (a type of liability). One example of this type of debt financing would be today's small residential building contractors. Typically, such contractors require a payment before beginning work and subsequent payments as construction progresses. Final payment is required on completion.

Another example would be the example of the law firm from Chapter 2. Prior to starting an engagement, Patrick J. Romano Jr. would require his clients to post a retainer. Once the retainer was used up, the client would be asked to replenish it before work was to be resumed. Some professionals in the service industry require clients to post a retainer equal to two or more months of anticipated services and then bill the actual services rendered every 30 days. The retainer acts like a security deposit and allows the firm to keep working on the project without interruption due to tardy payments.

In general, well-established professionals are paid before incurring costs. The first key is the reputation of the firm. The drawbacks are that a retainer or customer deposit may be inadequate. Second, the money allocated to a job may be spent on another job or some prior debts, thus undermining the purpose of the monies.

Equity

On its face, it would appear that equity would be the cheapest cost of funding. Looks can be deceiving, however. Equity is actually the

EXHIBIT 5.1 Average Rates of Returns for Years Ending 1926–2002*

Small Stocks	Large Stocks	Long-Term T-Bills	Intermediate-Term T-Bills	T-Bills	Inflation
17.7%	12.0%	5.7%	5.4%	3.8%	3.1%

*Information was taken from Bodie, Kane, and Marcus, *Investments* (New York: McGraw-Hill).

most costly form of funding. A careful review of Exhibit 5.1 bears this out. The exhibit omits the average corporate borrowing rate because of the diversity of loan products. Nevertheless, the average borrowing rates for 1926 to 2002 are less than the average rates of return for large stocks and higher than the average rate of returns for long-term Treasury bills.

Exhibit 5.1 does not address the average rate of returns for small privately held companies. According to some studies, small privately held businesses have experienced an average rate of return in excess of 35 percent. These average rates of return are indicative of the minimum rate of return an investor will require, given the amount of risk in each of the aforementioned categories. Equity investment can be divided into two categories, public and nonpublic. As we can see from the exhibit, if equity is used to fund the project, the cost could actually be a great deal higher than if debt is used.

A public company is one whose securities are registered with the SEC. Accordingly, public companies must abide by a plethora of rules and regulations. In addition, all of the company's financial data and pertinent information, such as executive compensation, are available to the general public. Hence the term "public company."

Conversely, a nonpublic company's financial information and other pertinent information are not available to the public. In some cases, this information may not even be available to minority shareholders.

In either the public or nonpublic arena, there can be voting and nonvoting stock. Voting stockholders get a say in how things are done at the company; nonvoting stockholders do not. In addition, there can be common stock or preferred. Preferred stock has a designated fixed dividend attached to it, and its dividends are paid before common stock dividends.

In all cases, shareholders have rights and can take legal action against the board of directors for not running the company properly. Shareholder rights vary from state to state.

The cost of funding a project with equity is the amount of value that is given up to the new investor. Earlier we discussed the required rate of returns of investors. Public companies must go through the expense of filing registration disclosure statements with and having them approved by the SEC.

A nonpublic company should prepare what is called a private placement memorandum (PPM). The PPM does not have to be filed with any regulatory authorities, but it serves the purpose of staving off lawsuits from disgruntled investors. Many attorneys believe that if a company is not required to register with the SEC, then it is not subject to securities laws on the state level. Their position is incorrect; be sure to seek out a securities lawyer for assistance.

In addition to the costs outlined, an underwriter may be involved. Underwriting fees and expenses can range from 5 percent to 15 percent of the money raised.

Income Tax Effect

As the old saying goes, only two things are certain in life: death and taxes. Since income taxes take a large percentage of an organization's taxable income, they have to be considered with the cost of financing. Interest paid on loans or bonds is tax deductible. The costs associated with securing and closing these types of financing are deductible over the life of the financing. The ability to deduct for the payment of interest and related costs effectively reduces the amount of that cost when an organization has taxable income.

The costs of raising and securing common or preferred stock are not tax deductible; they reduce the organization's equity but not net income. Nor is the cash paid out as dividends deductible. In regard to Trade Debt and Customer Deposits (Retainers), a careful distinction must be made. Assuming the company reports on an accrual basis rather than a tax basis, certain businesses can elect to file their income tax returns on a cash basis as opposed to the accrual basis. The fundamental difference is that a cash basis recognizes the income or expense when physically received or paid. Accrual basis recognizes income when earned and deducts expenses when incurred.

The incurrence of trade debt or customer deposits (retainers) has tax implications, but their magnitude does not. For example, Organization 1 and Organization 2, with identical reporting periods, identical gross income, and identical net income, could report $100,000 in total expenses. At the end of their reporting periods, Organization 1 could have no trade debt and Organization 2 could have $50,000 in trade debt. The amount of trade debt or the lack thereof would have no impact on income taxes. The effect on taxes has to do with the timing of when the expense is incurred and not with the liability of that expense. The same is true of customer deposits (retainer arrangements).

Cost Implications of the Funding Methodology

Chapter 2 explained that by increasing the organization's profitability, activity, and leverage ratios, an increase in return on equity would occur and that ratio analysis would be supplemented with EVA (economic value added) and MVA (market value added) analysis. Here is the tie-in, which contains the foundation for creating value. When sane investors buy stock, they do so with the expectation of making money. Each share of stock represents a right to a percentage of the company's assets and net income.

Theoretically, investors pay a price for a share of stock with an expectation of the percentage increase in the respective asset value (increase in stock price) and a respective share of income stream (dividend payout). In other words, investors are anticipating some combination of stock price appreciation or dividend payout. A company that sells a percentage of its company has to forgo a percentage of its asset appreciation and its income streams. That percentage is referred to as a company's cost of capital.

A company's assets are financed with either debt or equity. In today's world of finance, almost all companies have debt. That debt component has a cost associated with it as well, called interest expense. If a company's assets are financed with debt and equity, it is important to know the percentage of each relative to total assets.

The sum of the percentage of equity and debt multiplied by their respective costs is called the weighted average cost of capital (WACC). It is extremely important to note that in reference to WACC, the debt component includes only interest-bearing debt. The company's debt and its equity is also called its capital structure.

In addition, if a company has preferred stock, then its weight and cost becomes a third component of the WACC formula. Preferred stock is essentially treated as another form of debt. The weight for the preferred stock includes only the value in the preferred stock account. Retained earnings, additional paid-in capital, treasury stock, and common stock would be consolidated for consideration into the weight of equity. Exhibit 5.2 presents WACC in equation format for a company without preferred stock.

The underlying theory behind EVA and MVA is that there is a required operating profit from the business as a result of the equity and debt invested in the organization. That required operating profit as a

EXHIBIT 5.2 WACC Formula

WACC = (Weighted Percentage of Equity) (Cost of Capital)
     +(Weighted Percentage of Debt) (Cost of Debt)

percentage is equal to WACC. The amount of operating profit above or below the required amount either creates or destroys value, respectively.

The amount of return that is required is also called the hurdle rate, because in order to create value for the organization, the company must have a positive return greater than the company's WACC. In other words, a cost is associated with a company's equity and debt. A good manager needs to invest the company's equity or incur debt in projects that make more money than the cost of the money used to fund the company's assets. For illustrative purposes, refer to Exhibit 2.5.

In Exhibit 2.5, at the end of December 31, 2010, Pontrelli Recycling Inc. has $1,569,546 and $4,736,649 in interest-bearing debt and equity, respectively, for a total of $6,306,195. For the purpose of doing the WACC calculation, the weighted percentage of debt is 25 percent (1,569,546/6,306,195) and the weighted percentage of equity is 75 percent (4,731,593/6,306,195). It is important to note when performing the WACC calculation that you use the fair market value of debt and equity in the determination of the weights or percentages. In our example, we are assuming that the book value of debt and equity approximates their fair market value.

It is important to note that the sum of the percentages of debt and equity has to equal 100 percent. Later we discuss how to calculate the cost of debt and equity. For the purposes of this illustration only, the cost of capital will be 17 percent and the after-tax cost of debt will be 4.8 percent. Applying the weights and the costs to the formula in Exhibit 5.2, Exhibit 5.3 indicates that Pontrelli Recycling Inc. has a weighted average cost of capital of 13.95 percent. Therefore, the only way to create value for Pontrelli Recycling Inc. is to invest in projects that return greater than 13.95 percent.

EXHIBIT 5.3 WACC Formula Version 2

$$\text{WACC} = (75\%)\,(17\%) + (25\%)\,(4.8\%)$$
$$\text{WACC} = 12.75\% + 1.20\%$$
$$\text{WACC} = 13.95\%$$

EXHIBIT 5.4 EVA Formula

EVA = NOPAT − Capital Charge

This is the single most important concept in finance: Equity and debt alike have costs associated with them, and an investment in a project should be undertaken only if the expected returns are greater than the client's WACC. Accordingly, a project manager needs to be conscientious about the company's WACC and the return on a specific project.

Method for Calculating the Company's Cost of Funding

Economic value added (EVA) is defined as the difference of net operating profit after taxes (NOPAT) less the capital charge (CC) (see Exhibit 5.4).

Capital charge is defined as the product of WACC multiplied by the beginning balance of the company's capital or equity for the period under review (see Exhibit 5.5). EVA actually shows the amount of value that is created (or destroyed) by the company during the period of operation for which it is calculated.

Market value added (MVA) is defined as the market value of the company less the book value of the company (see Exhibit 5.6).

The market value of the company is defined simply as the market value of the equity and the debt. The book value of the company is the amount of equity and debt indicated on the company's balance sheet for the date being examined. The MVA calculation indicates the value created up until that date. It does not indicate the value created during the last period. To determine whether there has been an increase in MVA from one year to another, the MVA for the prior period

EXHIBIT 5.5 Capital Charge Formula

Capital Charge = WACC × Beginning Capital

EXHIBIT 5.6 MVA Formula

Market Value of the Company's Equity and Debt
$-$ Book Value of the Company's Equity and Debt
$=$ Market Value Added

---

will have to be calculated. After the prior period has been calculated, the percentage increase or decrease can be derived from the comparison.

MVA shows the amount of value that the stock market feels has been created or destroyed during the period of calculation, since MVA is based on a public company's stock price multiplied by the number of shares. There is a correlation of MVA to EVA. The MVA of a company is equal to the present value of the future EVA of the company (see Exhibit 5.7).

The major drawback for MVA is that the fair market value of the equity and debt is needed for the calculation. Typically, this information is available only for public companies. More often than not, public companies will have the financial expertise to calculate MVA. Accordingly, this chapter focuses on EVA.

Accounting for financial information is essentially dictated by generally accepted accounting principles (GAAP). The problem is that there are many options for recording many common transactions. This is not to say that the options don't have a very good basis. In fact, they do. The trouble is the choice of one option over another can have dramatically different effects on a company's financial statements. The issues with trying to compare financial statements have caused many non-accounting professionals to restate GAAP as

EXHIBIT 5.7 MVA Equation

$$MVA = \frac{EVA}{WACC - Constant\ Growth\ Rate}$$

---

creative reporting accounting principles, or CRAP. Obviously, the intricacies of accounting are lost on them.

EVA requires the preparer to adjust the financial statements to account for five scenarios:

1. Capitalizing leases
2. Use of first in, first out (FIFO)
3. Capitalizing research and development (R&D) costs
4. Adding back capital write-offs
5. Adding back goodwill amortization

The underling theory is that the five scenarios have the effect of understating assets and income. For example, all R&D costs for new products are expensed when incurred. A company spends money for R&D because it is trying to bring a new product or service to market. The company makes the decision to do this in the hopes of making money. In other words, the company spends the R&D monies for the purpose of making money in the future.

The future benefit is an asset. Accordingly, EVA theory believes that the R&D monies should be capitalized on the balance sheet (made an asset) and not expensed on the statement of operations. The effects of these adjustments are to recognize the inclusion of assets and the reduction of charges to the statement of operations. It's an attempt to recognize the true economic reality for value.

Exhibit 5.2 presents the formula for WACC. The mechanics are fairly simple: Multiply the weighted percentage of capital by the cost of capital and add the product of multiplying the weighted percentage of debt by the after-tax cost of debt. Calculating the weighted percentages of equity and debt is also easy. Using the balance sheets from Exhibits 2.5 and 2.6 will illustrate how easy it is.

Exhibit 5.8 presents the total interest-bearing debt and equity taken from Exhibits 2.5 and 2.6 for the year ending December 31, 2010. The debt for Pontrelli Recycling Inc. is comprised of Notes Payable (Short Term) of $440,318 and Notes Payable (Long Term) of

EXHIBIT 5.8 Total Debt and Equity

	Pontrelli Recycling, Inc.		Patrick J. Romano Jr. P.C.	
Debt	$ 1,569,546	25%	$ -0-	0%
Equity	$ 4,736,649	75%	$ 128,421	100%
Total	$ 6,306,195	100%	$ 128,421	100%

$1,129,228 for a total of $1,569,546. The issue is much easier for Patrick J. Romano Jr., P.C., because the law firm has no debt. In this instance the cost of equity will equal the WACC.

The percentages indicated in Exhibit 5.8 are just a function of dividing debt or equity by total debt and equity. There are only two wrinkles here. The first is that the cost of debt to borrow at current rates should be selected as opposed to historical rates. The cost to borrow at current rates more aptly reflects the environment in which the future investment will be made.

The second wrinkle is that very often there are more costs associated with borrowing than interest expense. It is hoped that these ancillary costs will prove to be immaterial. Examples of ancillary costs include application fees, loan origination fees, recording fees, both lender and borrower legal fees, higher insurance thresholds, and increased financial statement reporting. In addition to these costs, borrowing on real estate can involve fees for surveying, title insurance, and environmental issues. These costs should be added to the interest expense in order to arrive at the actual cost of the money borrowed.

A quick inquiry to the finance department, president, or the lender should provide the information needed. A word of caution is warranted here: Although lenders will definitely be cognizant of the fees and rates, they will not necessarily know some of the ancillary costs just mentioned. A joint meeting with the lender and the lender's underwriting department should fill in most of the gaps. After

EXHIBIT 5.9 After Tax Cost of Debt Equation

After-Tax Cost of Debt = (Cost of Debt) × (1 − Effective Tax Rate)

$$4.8\% \quad = \quad (8\%) \times (1 - .399)$$

completing the calculation for the cost of debt, you must calculate the debt at its after-tax cost for the purposes of WACC.

Chapter 2 explained how to calculate the company's effective tax rate. The cost of borrowing in the 2010 year for Pontrelli Recycling, Inc. before taxes is 8 percent. Exhibit 2.2 indicates that its effective tax rate is 39.9 percent. Exhibit 5.9 provides the formula and the calculation for the after-tax cost of debt for Pontrelli Recycling, Inc. in 2010.

If the company issues bonds, you will need to work with the yield to maturity as opposed to the coupon rate.

The preceding discussion illustrates that the calculation for three of the four variables in the WACC equation are fairly direct. The calculation for the cost of equity is a horse of a different color. If the company has had a recent business valuation performed by a qualified professional, then that valuation should have yielded a capitalization of earnings rate. The capitalization of earnings rate should be the equivalent to WACC. If you know what WACC equals, the weights of equity and debt, and the after-tax cost of debt, you should be able to calculate the cost of capital. The formula is represented in Exhibit 5.10.

Exhibit 5.11 uses the data from Exhibit 5.3 and the formula from Exhibit 5.10.

Exhibit 5.12 presents a formula for calculating the cost of capital when there has been no valuation. That formula is called the capital

EXHIBIT 5.10 Cost of Capital Equation

$$\frac{\text{WACC} - [(\text{Weight of Debt}) (\text{After-Tax Cost of Debt})]}{\text{Weight of Equity}} = \text{Cost of Capital}$$

EXHIBIT 5.11 Cost of Capital Percentage

$$\frac{13.95\% - [(25\%)\,(4.8\%)]}{75\%} = 17\%$$

asset pricing model (CAPM). There are literally thousands of articles on CAPM. In addition, there are a lot of sophisticated math and graphic explanations. There is no need for anxiety; this book aims to give you a practical working knowledge of CAPM.

The easiest component to ascertain in the CAPM formula is the risk-free rate. The risk-free rate is related to what the United States Treasury will pay you on its 3-month Treasury bill or 10-year Treasury bond. This is not to say that the two rates are identical. In actuality, they are rarely the same. In practice, most overseas companies use the 3-month Treasury bill. Most U.S. companies use the 10-year Treasury bond rate.

The rates for these bonds are listed in newspaper stock pages. Most search engines that offer financial resources will be able to supply the rates as well. For the purpose of this book, it is recommended that you use the 3-month Treasury bill rate. For the purpose of this book, we will use a ratio as of December 31, 2010 of 4.3 percent.

The second easiest component is the market premium. Market premium is defined as the average amount of return the entire stock market has returned over and above the risk-free rate. The historical average for market premium is between 7 percent and 8 percent. It is important to note that the historical average represents the growth of our nation from an agricultural economy to a manufacturing economy and transitioning from technology to a service economy. Given

EXHIBIT 5.12 Cost of Capital Equation

Cost of Capital = Risk-Free Rate + (Relative Risk of the Company)
× (Market Premium)

the current standard of living, it would be very difficult to match this kind of growth going forward. In addition, historical inflation in the United States has been 3.5 percent. Many experts recommend using 5 percent as the market premium going forward in light of these facts. Deriving the remaining component requires some work.

The relative risk of the company is called its beta equity coefficient. Beta is an index that relates to the relative risk of the company and its industry outlook. In other words, the beta equity coefficient shows how a company has reacted to historical market conditions. A lower beta means that the company is less volatile or risky, while a higher beta indicates higher risk or volatility. When the market is rapidly rising, the company with the higher beta will likely rise more quickly. In a falling market, the higher beta will drop more quickly.

Most public companies have published betas. If the company in question is a public company, then chances are there is an army of internal finance people who know what both the beta and the cost of capital are. Otherwise, there is a way to estimate what beta should be.

When attempting to calculate beta, there are a couple of things to keep in mind. The ideal thing to do is to find a company whose beta is published and that is in the exact same industry that the company you are working with is in. In finance vernacular, finding this like company that sells similar products is referred to as finding the pure play.

You may be presented with two problems. The first is a result of all of today's conglomerates. An example would be Pepsi-Co Inc. It is in the beverage and snack food businesses. It might be difficult to find a like company that is in the exact same industries. If a pure play isn't readily identifiable, then you need to select a company that has similar business processes and product life cycles and responds similarly to changes in the market.

The second problem that you will encounter is the capital structures. Some companies have different debt-to-equity ratios. The more debt a company has, the higher the beta. The underlying theory is that increased debt implies greater mandatory cash flow demands on operations. Hence fixed expenses are higher. The increased fixed expenses elevate the company's breakeven point.

A company with a higher breakeven point is more risky than a similar company with a lower breakeven point. In addition, capital always costs more than debt. At first glance it would appear that a company should maximize its debt in order to create a low WACC. The lower the WACC, the easier it is to find projects that make sense and the easier it is to create value. Unfortunately, more debt (risk in this case) causes the cost of capital to go up by way of the increased magnitude of the beta coefficient.

Due to the relationship of debt and risk (reflected by way of the beta coefficient), the amount of equity versus debt has no effect on WACC. This theory belongs to two smart guys named Modigliani and Miller, referred to as the M and M boys of finance. (They are not to be confused with the M and M boys of baseball, Mantle and Maris, or with Hershey's candies.)

In order to understand what a beta should be in a company without debt, you need to unlever the beta. To unlever a beta means to adjust it to a capital structure with no debt. A company's beta with its given level of debt is specifically called beta equity. A company's beta with no debt is called its beta asset. The idea is to take the pure play's beta equity and convert it to its beta asset, then adjust the pure play's beta asset for your client's given level of debt in order to arrive at your client's beta equity.

There are at least two schools of thought on how to convert beta equity to beta asset. One theory is to multiply beta equity by the market value weight of equity (see Exhibit 5.13). This theory assumes that there are no income taxes.

EXHIBIT 5.13 Beta Asset Equation Version 1

Beta Asset = Beta Equity × Market Value Weight of Equity

EXHIBIT 5.14 Beta Asset Equation Version 2

$$\text{Beta Asset} = \frac{\text{Beta Equity}}{1 + \{(1 - \text{Tax Rate}) \times (\text{Market Value Debt/Market Value Equity})\}}$$

The second theory divides beta equity by one plus the product of the benefit of the tax shield of the interest payments multiplied by the market values of the debt to equity ratio (see Exhibit 5.14). This theory assumes no default risk on the debt.

Modern theorists believe that both equations are wrong because of inadequacies in their assumptions. They also believe that the truth lies in between the two theories. Today's reality has income taxes and considers the default risk of debt. For purposes of this discussion, it is recommended that you use the formula in Exhibit 5.13 for two reasons: It penalizes the use of debt because of the risk of default, and it is easier to calculate.

For illustration purposes, a hypothetical public company named ARC Inc., a recycling company out of Indiana, has been identified as a pure play for Pontrelli Recycling, Inc. Its beta equity is 2.2 and its market value weight of equity is 86.6 percent. The first step is to calculate the beta asset using the formula in Exhibit 5.13 with ARC Inc.'s given data (see Exhibit 5.15).

The next step is to calculate Pontrelli Recycling's beta equity. A reminder is warranted here. ARC Inc. is a public company. Pontrelli Recycling is not a public company. In addition, the market value of its equity is also unknown. As stated earlier, use the market values when they are known. If the market values are unknown, then use the book values. Accordingly, the weighted book value of equity for Pontrelli Recycling is 75 percent.

EXHIBIT 5.15 Beta Asset Equation with Calculations

Beta Asset = Beta Equity × Market Value Weight of Equity
   1.905   =   2.2   × 86.6%

EXHIBIT 5.16 Beta Equity Equation

$$\text{Beta Equity} = \frac{\text{Beta Asset}}{\text{Weight of Equity}} \quad \text{or} \quad 2.54 = \frac{1.905}{75\%}$$

Since ARC Inc. was selected as the pure play and its beta asset is 1.905, then Pontrelli Recycling's beta asset is 1.905. The formula in Exhibit 5.16 is recommended to convert beta asset to beta equity.

Once all three variables are known, the formula in Exhibit 5.12 can be used to calculate the cost of capital. Exhibit 5.17 illustrates the calculation of the cost of capital for Pontrelli Recycling, Inc. at December 31, 2010.

Conclusion

We have explained all of the underlying components for calculating EVA. Now it comes full circle back to the formula in Exhibit 5.4. Staying with the Pontrelli Recycling example, it is possible to test if EVA was created for 2010. The formula from Exhibit 5.4 is EVA = NOPAT − Capital Charge. The formula from Exhibit 5.5 is Capital Charge = WACC · Beginning Capital. Exhibit 5.3 indicates that the WACC for Pontrelli Recycling is 13.95 percent. Exhibit 2.5 indicates that beginning stockholders' equity was $3,055,166. Exhibit 5.18 indicates the calculation for capital charge.

The capital charge is the minimum amount of profit that your client should generate for the stockholders and lenders for the amount of risk undertaken in advancing monies for equity or debt.

EXHIBIT 5.17 Actual Cost of Capital Calculation

$$\text{Cost of Capital} = \text{Risk-Free Rate} + \left(\begin{array}{c} \text{Relative Risk} \\ \text{of the Company} \end{array} \right) \left(\begin{array}{c} \text{Market} \\ \text{Premium} \end{array} \right)$$

$$17\% \qquad = 4.3\% \qquad + \qquad (2.54 \times 5\%)$$

EXHIBIT 5.18 Capital Charge Equation and Calculation

Capital Charge $=$ WACC $\times$ Beginning Capital

$426,196 $\quad= 13.95\% \times \$3,055,166$

Accordingly, the project manager needs to be cognizant of this charge. The more the client makes over its capital charge, the more valuable the company becomes.

Exhibit 2.5 indicates that Pontrelli Recycling's net income for 2010 was $1,681,483. NOPAT is an acronym for net operating profit after taxes (before interest expense). A word of caution is warranted here. Remember that the after-tax cost of the debt is already accounted for in the capital charge through WACC. Net income includes interest accrued to the lenders in 2010. The reason for NOPAT is to avoid accounting for the interest accrued with its corresponding tax shield twice.

Exhibit 2.5 indicates that Pontrelli Recycling, Inc.'s income from operations was $2,945,079. Accordingly, this figure has to be tax affected in order to convert it to NOPAT. Given its 39.9 percent tax rate, NOPAT is $1,769,993 ($2,945,079 $\times$ (1 $-$ TR)). Inserting these numbers into the EVA calculation (Exhibit 5.19) indicates a positive result. A positive number indicates that EVA was created at Pontrelli Recycling during 2010. Conversely, if EVA had a negative result, then value would have been destroyed during 2010.

The idea of creating value is what fuels the phenomenon called capitalism. Your ability to shepherd or design a project that creates value for your client is probably the reason why you were hired to begin with.

A company's payment for assets has been provided by either equity or debt. Investors and lenders alike advance their money to a

EXHIBIT 5.19 EVA Calculation

$\quad$ EVA $=$ NOPAT $\quad-$ Capital Charge

$1,343,797 $= \$1,769,993 - \$426,196$

company for investment into these assets. Investors and lenders expect the company's assets to generate a return directly proportionate to the risk involved. A company's operations must yield more than the expected returns of investors and lenders in order to create value. Failure to do so destroys the value of the company. Project managers need to know how to calculate these costs in order to evaluate their clients and one alternative over another.

CHAPTER 6

Project Revenue and Cash Flows

Chapter 5 discussed calculating an enterprise-wide hurdle rate, weighted average cost of capital (WACC). This chapter looks at the investing and financing decisions on a company's individual projects. We provide insight on the role of the financial manager and introduce how to calculate a company's statement of cash flows. The statement of cash flows analysis will act as a segue into calculating free cash flows of a proposed project. Then we focus on different methodologies for calculating a project's viability.

Role of the Financial Manager

It is a common misconception that accountants are financial managers. The fundamental difference between accounting and finance is that accounting is the recording or categorizing of financial transactions for the purpose of constructing and interpreting financial statements. The purpose of finance is to develop benchmarks as a guide to managers. Titles like controller, treasurer, and chief financial officer often are used interchangeably, as are accountant and financial manager. The exact assignment of duties and responsibilities is determined by a company's individual uniqueness.

In order to avoid confusion, the project manager should consult the company's organization chart. It is important to note that people with impeccable accounting skills, such as certified public accountants (CPAs), do not necessarily have financial management knowledge or skills. A CPA's training is vastly different from that of a financial manager.

Accountants who have the proper financial training background can be quite adept financial managers. Once again, if the client is a large company with knowledgeable finance personnel, this chapter will serve as a guide for what questions to ask. If not, the information in this chapter will teach the project manager to calculate cash flows and project rates of return.

The role of a financial manager is to create an optimal balance sheet in order to generate maximum return for the company owners. Simply, a balance sheet is a snapshot of a business's assets, liabilities, and equity at the end of a given day. The assets on a balance sheet must equal the sum of its liabilities and equity. The beauty and foundation of accounting is that it is a double-entry system designed to insure that the debits and credits equal. Assets are debit balance accounts.

Liabilities and equity are credit balance accounts. The double-entry system provides a check and balance to signal mistakes in data entry. In keeping with the duality concept, the financial manager has two general types of decisions, investing and financing. Investing decisions encompass current and fixed assets. As indicated in Chapter 5, financing decisions encompass liabilities and equity.

Whether the financial manager is making investing or financing decisions, there must be a plan. The role of financial planning is to take expectations and translate them into a financial format, which includes three essential documents: a cash budget, a pro forma income statement, and a pro forma balance sheet. Before these financial formats are assembled, the manager must consider the corporate mission and strategic planning (see Chapter 1). Depending on the goal of the financial manager, the pro forma statements can be replaced with financial forecasts and financial projections. The distinction between the three will be elaborated on later.

Corporate mission and strategic planning must be incorporated into establishing strategic operating plans. Last but not least, a strategic "financial" plan has to be developed.

The role of a strategic financial plan is twofold. It communicates the plan, and it establishes metrics for measurement and control. It should be fairly obvious at this point that the importance of understanding the company's financial characteristics, strategic planning and processes, value creation, and how all of that fits together is paramount to being able to distinguish a better alternative from a bad one.

As indicated in Chapter 7, a cash budget is derived from a detailed operating plan. A pro forma income statement utilizes detailed operating plans and historical financial ratios. The historical financial ratios are used to anticipate gross profit margin, net profit margin, operating profit margin, tax rate, and operating expense ratio. The purpose of applying the ratios to projected results is to verify that the financial assumptions are correct (for example Inventory Turns, or Accounts Receivable Collection Period) and have been properly reflected in the detailed operating plan. The accuracy is usually dependent on the sales forecast.

A pro forma balance sheet uses the detailed operating plans, historical financial ratios, data from the pro forma income statement, and finally the effects on cash and debt. The historical financial ratios used to calculate balances on the pro forma balance sheet are total asset turnover ratio, fixed asset turnover ratio, net property plant and equipment ratio, other asset ratio, working capital ratio, inventory turnover ratio, days of inventory on hand ratio, accounts receivable collection period, and accounts payable collection period. The effects on cash and debt are addressed later in this chapter.

It is important to recognize how each financial format builds on one another with the detailed operating plan acting as the foundation. We cannot emphasize enough the importance of the word "detail" in regard to the detailed operating plan. Unless meticulous effort is put into the detailed operating plan, there is a high probability of a garbage in, garbage out scenario.

Another word of caution is warranted here in regard to semantics; back to accounting again. In accounting, there is a fundamental difference among a pro forma financial, a financial projection, and a financial forecast. According to "The AICPA Guide for Prospective Financial Information," issued by the American Institute of Certified Public Accountants, "pro forma" financial statements (income statement and balance sheet) are essentially historical financial statements adjusted for a prospective transaction.

The objective of some financial presentations, commonly called pro forma information, is to show what the significant effects on historical financial information might have been, had a consummated or proposed transaction (or event) occurred at an earlier date. The AICPA Guide defines financial forecasts as:

> . . . *prospective financial statements that present, to the best of the responsible party's knowledge and belief, an entity's expected financial position, results of operations, and cash flows.*
>
> *A financial forecast is based on the responsible party's assumptions reflecting conditions it expects to exist and the course of action it expects to take. A financial forecast may be expressed in specific monetary amounts as a single point estimate of forecasted results or as a range, where the responsible party selects key assumptions to form a range within it reasonably expects, to the best of its knowledge and belief, the item or items subject to the assumptions to actually fall. If a forecast contains a range, the range is not selected in a biased or misleading manner.*[1]

According to the AICPA Guide, financial projection is "prospective financial statements that present, to the best of the responsible party's knowledge and belief, given one or more hypothetical assumptions, an entity's expected financial position, results of operations and cash flows."[2] A financial projection is sometimes prepared to present one or more hypothetical courses of action for evaluation, as in response to a question that begins, for instance, "What would happen if . . . ?"

A financial projection is based on the reasonable party's assumptions reflecting conditions it expects would exist and the course of action it expects would be taken, given one or more hypothetical assumptions. A projection, like a forecast, may contain a range. It is important to keep in mind that these subtle distinctions apply to the world of public accounting. CPAs are bound by these distinctions. Everyone else is not. Nevertheless, it is a probably a good idea to follow the guidelines.

How to Calculate the Statement of Cash Flows for a Company

According to Professor John Halloran of the University of Notre Dame, the role of the statement of cash flows is to "provide information about magnitude and composition of a company's cash generating power." A statement of cash flows is prepared from the beginning of a company's fiscal year to the date presented. It never covers a period longer than one year. The statement of cash flows is part of any complete financial statement presentation. Accordingly, the AICPA has guidelines on presentation and disclosure.

This chapter focuses on the layperson's construction of the statement of cash flows, not on the CPA's requirements. Nevertheless, the two approaches are not dramatically different. The statement of cash flows essentially tells the reader what the company did with its cash. The statement is divided into three sections: operating activities, investing activities, and financing activities.

The operating activities section includes the results of the income statement, non-cash deductions such as depreciation and amortization, and changes in current assets and current liabilities. The investing activities section includes the purchasing or selling of fixed and other assets. The financing activities section includes the changes in debt and equity. Exhibit 6.1 shows how to set up a statement of cash flows.

Most of the lines in the exhibit contain the italicized words "increase," "decrease," "provided," or "used." When the words are in

EXHIBIT 6.1 Statement of Cash Flows

OPERATING ACTIVITIES

Net Income (Loss)
Adjustments:
    Depreciation and Amortization Expense
Additions:
    Accounts Receivable *(increase) decrease*
    Inventory *(increase) decrease*
    Prepaid Expenses *(increase) decrease*
    Accounts Payable *increase (decrease)*
    Taxes Payable *increase (decrease)*
    Customer Deposits *increase (decrease)*

Net Cash Flow *Provided (Used)* by Operating Activities

INVESTING ACTIVITIES

Net Property, Plant, and Equipment *(increase) decrease*
Other Assets *(increase) decrease*

Net Cash Flow *provided (Used)* by Investing Activities

FINANCING ACTIVITIES

Notes Payable *increase (decrease)*
Common Stock *increase (decrease)*

Net Cash Flow *Provided (Used)* by Financing Activities

CHANGE IN CASH

BEGINNING CASH

ENDING CASH

parentheses, the net change of the amount should be subtracted. For illustrative purposes, Exhibit 6.2 presents a statement of cash flows for Pontrelli Recycling, Inc. for the year ending December 31, 2010, utilizing the data in Exhibit 2.5. Pontrelli Recycling, Inc. was chosen

EXHIBIT 6.2 Sample Statement of Cash Flows

Pontrelli Recycling, Inc.
Statement of Cash Flows
For the Year Ending
December 31, 2010

Operating Activities

Line: 1	Net Income	$1,681,483
	Adjustments:	
Line: 2	Depreciation and Amortization	154,997
	Additions:	
Line: 3	Increase in Accounts Receivable	(1,081,295)
Line: 4	Decrease in Inventory	178,425
Line: 5	Prepaid Expenses	not applicable
Line: 6	Increase in Accounts Payable	232,417
Line: 7	Increase in Taxes Payable	84,595
Line: 8	Customer Deposits	not applicable
Line: 9	Net Cash Flow Provided by Operating Activities	$1,250,622
	Investing Activities	
Line: 10	Net Property, Plant, and Equipment	$ -0-
Line: 11	Decrease in Other Assets	22,708
Line: 12	Net Cash Flow Provided by Investing Activities	$ 22,708
	Financing Activities	
Line: 13	Decrease in Borrowings	$ (78,145)
Line: 14	Common Stock/Equity	-0-
Line: 15	Net Cash Flow Used by Financing Activities	$ (78,145)
Line: 16	Change in Cash	$1,195,185
Line: 17	Beginning Cash	2,254,815
Line: 18	Ending Cash	$3,450,000

over Patrick J. Romano Jr., P.C. because its balance sheet is more sophisticated and would provide a better illustration. In Exhibit 6.2, each line is numbered for easy reference.

In Exhibit 6.2, line 1 was derived from net income amount on the statement of operations in Exhibit 2.5. Depreciation and amortization indicated in line 2 also comes from that statement. Depreciation expense is usually found in the operating expenses. For the purpose of this book, the detail in the operating expenses was omitted. You will have to take the authors' word for this number.

Line 3 is derived from the balance sheets for the years ending December 31, 2010 and December 31, 2009. The balances given on December 31, 2009 are representative of the balances of those accounts at the close of business on December 31, 2009. This also tells us that these balances must be the same at the start of the next morning of business. Hence, they are the beginning balances for 2010. Accordingly, the increase or decrease in these accounts is the result of subtraction between the balances given on December 31, 2010 and December 31, 2009.

The accounts receivable balances are $1,645,827 and $564,532 on December 31, 2010 and 2009, respectively. It is apparent that the accounts receivable balance has increased during 2010. A quick review of Exhibit 6.1 indicates that an increase in accounts receivable should be reflected as a negative balance. The difference is $1,081,295. Hence, the result indicated in line 3.

You might ask why an increase in an asset is a use of cash and an increase in a liability is a source of cash? Earlier we mentioned that a balance sheet's total assets equal the sum of its liabilities and equity. In order to increase a balance sheet's total assets, an increase in liabilities or equity will be necessary. Cash is an asset. In order to increase cash, you have to increase liabilities and equity or liquidate other assets. Hence, an increase in a non-cash asset is a use of cash. A decrease in a non-cash asset is a source of cash. An increase in liabilities is a source of cash. Conversely, a decrease in liabilities is a use of cash.

If it is difficult to remember these rules, then refer to Exhibit 6.1. Lines 4 through 8 are calculated in the same manner as line 3. As indicated, lines 5 and 8 are not applicable to Pontrelli Recycling. Line 9 is just the sum of lines 1 through lines 8. Lines 10 and 14 are the only two lines that are not derived from the simple subtraction of beginning and ending balances.

In regard to net property, plant, and equipment, it is important to factor in that year's depreciation expense. Depreciation is an accounting and tax concept. The difference between an expense and an asset is that the benefit of the expense has been realized and will have no future benefit. An asset is expected to have a future benefit. Once an asset has no future benefit, it is expensed. A simple example would be the purchase of a piece of paper versus the purchase of a desk. Once the piece of paper is used, it has no future benefit. The desk, however, can be used over and over.

Depreciation allows a company to expense a portion of the cost of the desk over what it anticipates will be the desk's useful life of service to the company. Note that there are set useful lives for certain types of assets. For example, a computer is expected to last 5 years, and a desk is expected to last 7 years. In reality, the computer will probably last 3 years and the desk 15 years. If an asset does not last the duration of its expected life, it is written off ahead of schedule. If an asset lasts longer than its expected life, then the company just continues to enjoy the benefits of it use.

Getting back to line 10, net property, plant, and equipment was depreciated for 2010 (see line 2). When calculating the increase and decrease in net property, plant, and equipment, you have to take into account the depreciation expense. Line 2 indicates that the amount of the depreciation is $154,997. The difference in beginning net property plant and equipment is $154,997.

In addition, the statement of operations does not indicate any gain or loss on the sale or disposal of assets. By process of deduction, there were no purchases or sales of net property, plant, and equipment. Of course there is an easier way to figure out whether property, plant, and equipment was purchased or disposed of; you could ask management. Line 11 is calculated in the same way as lines 3 through 8. Line 12 is the sum of lines 10 and 11. Line 13 is calculated in the same fashion as lines 3 through 8 and 11. As indicated earlier, line 14, equity, is not much different from net property, plant, and equipment. In the latter, though, you have to factor the depreciation into the change in the balances.

In equity, you have to factor in the year's net income or loss adjusted for distributions. The characterization of distributions depends on the legal structure of the company: S-corporation, C-corporation, partnership, limited liability company, or sole proprietorship. S-corporations call distributions previously taxed income distributions. C-corporations call them dividends. Partnerships call them partner draws. Limited liability companies call them member distributions, and sole proprietorships call them draws.

No matter what the distributions are called, you need to adjust the current year's income. In the example, Pontrelli Recycling's net income was $1,681,483. Beginning equity was $3,055,166. If you add beginning equity with this year's net income, then you arrive at an adjusted equity of $4,736,649. If you compare the adjusted equity to the end of the year's equity in this example, you will note that there is no change. Hence the zero value on line 14. Line 15 is the sum of lines 13 and 14. Line 16 is the sum of lines 9, 12, and 15. Line 17 is the ending cash value on the December 31, 2009, balance sheet. Line 18 is the sum of lines 16 and 17. The value on line 18 should equal the ending cash value on the balance sheet at December 31, 2010. This will become the proof as to whether the statement of cash flows was prepared correctly or not. Do not be alarmed if your calculations are off a dollar or two. This is usually the result of rounding.

Now that you are an expert in the preparation of the statement of cash flows, the next question should be: How is it helpful? There are a couple of dimensions to the answer. From the 32,000-foot view, the statement of cash flows tells you whether your company creates (provides) or burns (uses) cash. As you drill down further, it should be fairly easy to determine whether operating activities, investing activities, and financing activities provide or use cash.

Exhibit 6.2 indicates that the operating activities provide a great deal of cash, whereas the investing and financing activities are fairly insignificant. It is important to understand that the creation of cash from operating activities coupled with strong earnings is a good sign. In the exhibit, Pontrelli Recycling reported net income of $1,681,483 and depreciation of $154,997 for an adjusted net income of $1,836,480. The net cash provided from operating activities is $1,250,622. This indicates that the growth in sales had to be partially supplemented with an increase in assets, specifically accounts receivable, to the tune of $1,081,295.

A financial ratio analysis on the activity ratios over the last two years would shed some more light as to whether the company was increasing or decreasing those ratios. The increased efficiency or the impairment of these ratios may tell a story in themselves, but it may be the link to another answer. Increasing activity ratios will increase cash flows from operating activities. In addition, as described in Chapter 2, it will lead to an increase in profitability.

A use of cash in investing activities indicates that the company is making expenditures for hard assets, such as property, plant, and equipment. It could also mean that the company is making expenditures in other assets of an intangible nature. Intangible assets are usually intellectual property or goodwill. A word of caution is warranted here. Be very skeptical about intangible assets. An intangible asset creates value in its ability to generate future profits. If the intangible assets do not look like they are going to generate a reasonable profit for the investment, then they are probably not as valuable as indicated.

A real-life example of this was the WorldCom scenario. Apparently, WorldCom extended trade credit to unworthy customers. Just before these customers filed bankruptcy, WorldCom arranged a purchase of the nearly defunct entity in exchange for the outstanding accounts receivables. When a company has a bad debt on the books, it is required to write it off and take a charge to operations. Instead of reporting a bad debt on the books, WorldCom capitalized the accounts receivable as goodwill. The net result was that WorldCom's net income and assets were overstated.

Eventually, WorldCom owned so many unprofitable companies that its cash dried up. The overstatements of net income and goodwill made it appear that the company was a stellar performer and caused many investors to buy its stock. Needless to say, the public's investment was wiped out and the masterminds of the scheme have been sentenced to prison. A careful review of WorldCom's balance sheet and statement of cash flows would have indicated tremendous growth in goodwill and a large use of cash in investing activities, which should have tipped off stock analysts.

Another issue that deserves mentioning is when cash is provided by investing activities. Cash provided from investing activities indicates that the company is selling off its assets. Once again, it is important to prepare a "cross-trend" financial ratio analysis in order to supplement how the company is faring in its performance relative to its investment activity.

The financing activity section indicates how the company is funding its operating and investing activities. Ideally a company should provide cash from operating activities, use a portion of cash for investing activities, and use cash for distributions to the owners while retaining adequate levels of cash for operations. A company that is providing cash through financing activities and using cash to fund net operating losses and increased other operating activities is not healthy. As indicated in Chapter 5, there has to be consideration to the correct mix of debt versus equity in regard to optimizing WACC.

It is important to note that there is no magic combination of cash provided by operating, investing, and financing activities. The only certainty is that you cannot run a business without cash; a company must have cash. Generally speaking, more cash is better. Careful consideration has to be given as to the company's cost of excess cash to the owners of the equity or the debt. If an owner is anticipating a 20 percent return on their investment and the company has an excess of cash on hand, the company would be foolish to pay 20 percent for cash it did not need. The correct combination has to be determined based on the company's strategic plan, its financial ratio levels, and the financing of its projects.

Free Cash Flows

Free cash flow is defined as the amount of cash generated from a company's operating activities and investing activities plus the after-tax cost of the interest expense. These amounts are derived from the statement of cash flows. Earlier we mentioned that the AICPA's version of the statement of cash flows is slightly different from the one presented in Exhibit 6.1. One of those differences is that the interest and income tax expenses for the period reported are footnoted at the bottom of the AICPA statement.

Accordingly, you would take the interest expense figure and subtract the tax deduction for that expense. Remember, calculating the effective tax rate is as simple as dividing the income taxes by the sum of net income and the income taxes.

The amount of free cash flows is a determinant of value of a company. The greater the magnitude of the free cash flows, the more valuable the company becomes. This is a different perspective from Chapter 5, where economic value added (EVA) measures the value created or lost on a year-by-year basis.

If a statement of cash flows is not readily available, finance academics have come up with formulas for shortcutting the process. Exhibit 6.3 provides the formula and the key for the abbreviations.

EXHIBIT 6.3 Free Cash Flows

FCF = OCF – Change in NWC – CAPEX

FCF = Free Cash Flows

OCF = Operating Cash Flows

NWC = Net Working Capital

CAPEX = Capital Expenditures

EXHIBIT 6.4 Operating Cash Flows Equation

OCF = EBIT(1 − Tax Rate) + Depreciation

Operating cash flows is defined as the after-tax annual earnings before interest expense and taxes (EBIT) plus depreciation. The formula is shown in Exhibit 6.4.

As indicated earlier, operating cash flows is essentially lines 1 and 2 of Exhibit 6.2, with the adjustment of adding the income taxes and the net tax cost of the interest expense. The change in net working capital is essentially the sum of lines 3 through 8 in Exhibit 6.2. Capital Expenditures for fixed assets are essentially line 12 in that exhibit.

It is important to understand how to calculate free cash flows because this is the pool of money for which a project will be competing. The tougher competition, however, is the owners of the equity and the debt. The trick is to make better use of those monies in a project that will create more value than in the hands of the equity or debt owners.

Methods for Calculating a Project's Viability

How do you value the financial merits of one project over another? In theory, the investment value models that are used for valuing securities should also be used for valuing capital investments (projects). The problem is that securities are traded in markets like the New York Stock Exchange and NASDAQ. These markets are considered to be efficient for the most part. It is generally accepted that the price (cost) of a security equals its value. There is no efficient market for the buying and selling of projects.

In addition, many projects are predominantly one of a kind or unique. Therefore, there is no relation to the cost (price) of a project and its value. The process of financial evaluation of alternative projects is called capital budgeting. The objective of a project is to create an asset that will in turn create future value. That future value is expected to increase free cash flows.

In his book titled *Analysis for Financial Management*, Robert C. Higgins indicates that there are three steps to financial evaluation.[3] The first step is to establish "relevant cash flows," which is very much like the budgeting process addressed in Chapter 7. Relevant cash flows should include only incremental after-tax free cash flows. When preparing the relevant cash flows, you should consider how the execution and implementation of the project will affect the company's cash flows. Hence the use of the word "relevant" in describing the cash flows.

In addition, there are five recommended considerations in calculating relevant cash flows:

1. Self-generated working capital
2. Sunk costs
3. Allocated expenses
4. Excess capacity
5. Financing costs

Self-generating working capital, or spontaneous capital, refers to the fact that as a project begins there will be an opportunity to fund a portion of it with noninterest-bearing debt, such as accounts payable and taxes payable.

It is important to remember that these sources of cash have to be counterweighed against the requirements of current assets including, but not limited to, accounts receivable and inventory. Sunk costs are expenditures that have already been made and cannot be undone whether the project goes forward or not. Accordingly, they should not be included in the calculations of relevant cash flow.

Allocated expenses are similar to sunk costs. Allocated expenses are usually overhead expenses that the company apportions to its different operating segments, projects, or divisions. If these expenses exist and the company is going to have them whether the project happens or not, then they should not be included in the "relevant cash flows" calculation.

Excess capacity describes resources that are not going to cost the company any more money whether a project happens or not. If a particular project is going to exclude another project, then the cost of excess capacity would be included in the calculation of relevant cash flows. Otherwise the costs that are a result of absorbing the costs due to excess capacity should be omitted from the calculation.

The last consideration to be omitted from the calculation is financing costs. Later in the chapter we discuss using hurdle rates for a required return on a project. The required rate of return will involve a discount rate. The discount rate will take into consideration the costs of debt and equity. Accordingly, the cost of financing is already accounted for in the discount rate.

The second step in financial evaluation is to calculate a figure of merit, which means that you need to calculate a project's economic value. It is very important to remember that the three key aspects of investment returns are the size of the cash flow, the timing of the cash flow, and the risk of receiving the cash flow. In regard to size, it is intuitive.

The larger the amount of cash received, the better the investment. The question of timing has to do with the time value of money. Simply stated, a dollar today is worth more than a dollar in 10 years. There are three reasons for this. One is the risk of inflation. It is easily ascertainable what a dollar can buy today. It is not so easy to be certain what a dollar will buy in 10 years.

The second issue is the risk of something unexpected happening over the next 10 years that will prevent payment. The third issue is the loss of the opportunity to invest in another project over the next 10 years. The last key aspect of investment returns is the risk associated with the project's propensity for success.

Examples of figures of merit include accounting rate of return, payback period, net present value, internal rate of return, and

EXHIBIT 6.5 Accounting Rate of Return Equation

$$\text{Accounting Rate of Return} = \frac{\text{Annual Average Cash Inflows}}{\text{Total Cash Outflows}}$$

benefit-cost ratio. The formula for calculating the accounting rate of return is shown in Exhibit 6.5. The formula for calculating payback period is shown in Exhibit 6.6.

The advantages of these formulas are that they are familiar and simple to understand. The major disadvantages are that they ignore the different levels of risk for an individual project and ignore the timing of the returns. Exhibit 6.7 shows two projects with identical total cash outflows and annual average cash inflows. The total cash outflows consist of a one-time up-front payment of $60,000 and annual average cash inflows of $25,000 ($100,000/4 years).

Both projects will yield exactly the same results when applied to the formulas for accounting rate of return and payback period. Clearly, Project B promises to return a greater amount of cash sooner than Project A. Hence, neither formula addresses the value of receiving more cash in the earlier part of the project. Second, can you tell which project is more likely to succeed or not? The inability to distinguish which project is riskier is the second drawback to these formulas. The inability to value the timing of the payments and to quantify the risk of the individual project disregards two of the three key aspects of investment returns.

Accounting rate of return and payback period are said to be non-discounted cash flow oriented. The concept of discounting cash flow is to place a value on what a payment in the future is worth in today's dollars. The idea of discounting the value of money in the

EXHIBIT 6.6 Payback Period Equation

$$\text{Payback Period} = \frac{\text{Total Cash Outflows}}{\text{Annual Average Cash Inflows}}$$

EXHIBIT 6.7 Sample Total Cost Outflows

Year	Project A	Project B
1	$ 5,000	$ 50,000
2	$ 10,000	$ 30,000
3	$ 10,000	$ 10,000
4	$ 75,000	$ 10,000
Total	$100,000	$100,000

Note: Both projects have a one time only "upfront" cash flow of $60,000.

future is the inverse of the compounding of interest. The basic difference is that with compounding, the value of what we have today is known. The question becomes how much is today's money worth tomorrow, given an expected rate of return or interest rate.

In discounting the value of money, the value of a payment tomorrow is known. In discounting, the question becomes how much is tomorrow's money worth today, given an expected rate of return. Mathematicians have created present value tables that have annual percentages across the top and various periods along the side in ascending order. In each column is a decimal number, the present value factor.

For example, if you wanted to know what the value of $100,000 received four years from now is worth today with an expected return of 12 percent, then you would go to the present value tables and find the present value factor at the intersection of 12 percent and four periods. At that intersection, you would find the present value factor of 0.636. In order to determine the present value of the $100,000, you would multiply the $100,000 by 0.636 to arrive at a present value of $63,600. It is a rather simple process.

When there are payments at more frequent intervals than once a year, the calculation gets complicated. For illustrative purchases, the 12 percent expected rate of return will be applied to the two projects in Exhibit 6.7. Exhibit 6.8 includes the present value factors for periods 1 through 4 for an expected return of 12 percent.

EXHIBIT 6.8 Present Value Factors

Periods	PV Factor for 12%
1	0.893
2	0.797
3	0.712
4	0.636

Exhibit 6.9 illustrates the application of the present value factors to the projects in Exhibit 6.7.

If the risk is equal between Project A and Project B, then it is fairly easy to see that Project B is a superior investment to Project A. Exhibit 6.9 is the perfect example of how the time value of money affects the return on the investment in a project. This concept of applying the time value of money to an investment or project

EXHIBIT 6.9 Present Value Factors Applied to Projects A and B

				Project A			
Year	Payoff			PV Factor			Present Value of Payoff
1	$ 5,000	×	0.893	=			$ 4,465
2	$ 10,000	×	0.797	=			$ 7,970
3	$ 10,000	×	0.712	=			$ 7,120
4	$ 75,000	×	0.636	=			$47,700
Total	$100,000						$67,255

				Project B			
Year	Payoff			PV Factor			Present Value of Payoff
1	$ 50,000	×	0.893	=			$44,650
2	$ 30,000	×	0.797	=			$23,910
3	$ 10,000	×	0.712	=			$ 7,120
4	$ 10,000	×	0.636	=			$ 6,360
Total	$100,000						$82,040

EXHIBIT 6.10 Net Present Value Equation

Net Present Value = Present Value of Payoffs − Present Value of Costs

valuation is called the discounted cash flow criteria. The figures of merit that utilize discounted cash flow criteria are net present value, internal rate of return, and benefit-cost ratio.

Net present value is the comparison of the present value of the payoffs less the present value of the costs of the project. If the present values of the payoffs exceed the present value of the costs, then it is a project that creates value. Later in this chapter we discuss how to select a project when you have more favorable projects than resources and how to choose one project over another when they are mutually exclusive. Exhibit 6.10 represents net present value in equation format.

Earlier it was indicated that both Projects A and B had an initial one-time cost of $60,000. The present value of up-front payments or receipts is the amount paid or received. When payments are incurred during the project, then you apply the net present value factors in the same fashion as the exercise followed in present-valuing the payoffs (see Exhibit 6.9). It is important to remember that the payoffs, costs, and the timing of both are taken from the budget (see Chapter 7).

The math needed to calculate net present value is easy: Simply plug your payoffs and costs into the equations. The hard part is how to choose a discount rate. The discount rate is also called the company's required rate of return. In Chapter 5 it was established that in order to create value for the company, the company had to invest in projects that yielded a return greater than its weighted average cost of capital (WACC). One of the components of WACC is the cost of capital. Exhibit 6.10 presents the formula for the cost of capital.

A component of the formula measures the relative risk of the company. Measuring the relative risk of an individual project is another story. There are three scientific approaches for gauging a project's risk: sensitivity analysis, scenario analysis, and simulations. The details of these approaches are beyond the scope of this book. However, the point of going through one of these approaches is to identify the factors and scenarios that will affect the outcome of the project. These analyses may present new issues that can be reengineered in the project in order to mitigate an unexpected or undesirable outcome. After the issues have been identified, the next step is to apply weights to the likelihood of these events occurring.

Finally, there is a composite scoring followed with a benchmarking of safe, risky, and very risky categories. A safe project should be given the required rate of return equal to WACC. A risk premium should be applied in ascending order to the risky and very risky category. It is important to remember that although the formulas and theories have a scientific basis, it is impossible to quantify every benefit or cost associated with every project.

Internal rate of return is defined in terms of net present value (NPV). Internal rate of return is equal to the discount rate at which the investment's NPV equals zero. The calculated internal rate of return is then compared to the company's required rate of return. The risk of the project is compensated in the discount rate or required rate of return selected in the net present value calculation.

The last figure of merit is the benefit-cost ratio, defined as the ratio of the present value of cash inflows divided by the present value of the cash outflows. Exhibit 6.11 presents the formula.

The third step in financial evaluation is to come up with an "acceptance criterion" for giving the go-ahead on a project. The acceptance criterion is the minimum result the company will accept from a figure of merit. As indicated earlier, it is not practical to use the

EXHIBIT 6.11 Benefit-Cost Ratio

$$\text{Benefit-Cost Ratio} = \frac{\text{Present Value of Cash Inflows}}{\text{Present Value of Cash Outflows}}$$

accounting rate of return or payback period as a figure of merit. The choices for figures of merit are net present value, internal rate of return, and benefit-cost ratio. The criteria for acceptance or rejection of a project based on the figures of merit follow.

- *Net Present Value (NPV)*. If NPV is equal to or greater than zero, the project should be accepted. If NPV is less than zero, the project should be rejected.
- *Internal Rate of Return (IRR)*. If IRR is equal to or greater than the required rate of return, the project should be accepted. If IRR is less than the required rate of return, the project should be rejected.
- *Benefit-Cost Ratio (BCR)*. If BCR is greater than one, the project should be accepted. If BCR is less than one, the project should be rejected.

These guidelines would be great except that in the real world, companies do not have unlimited resources. The notion of having more favorable projects than resources requires capital rationing, which means allocating the inadequate amount of dollars available to the projects that will yield the best results. In addition, some projects preclude a company from taking on other projects because they are mutually exclusive.

To further complicate matters, some projects have unequal lives for comparison purposes. Navigating these issues is called capital budgeting. Accordingly, academics have developed a ranking system for choosing one figure of merit over another for competing projects. See Exhibit 6.12 for ranking priorities.

NPV is always chosen over IRR. Both figures of merit indicate whether a project is going to create or destroy value. NPV calculates how much value is going to be added, whereas IRR indicates a resulting rate of return on a project. Accordingly, net present value seems to be the choice for the figure of merit.

EXHIBIT 6.12 Ranking Priorities

Scenario Analysis	Ranking Method
Projects are totally independent of each other with ample resources.	Rank by Net Present Value, Internal Rate of Return, or Benefit-Cost Ratio.
Projects are mutually exclusive with equal lives.	Rank by the highest Net Present Value.
Projects are mutually exclusive with unequal lives.	Rank by the highest Net Present Value over a common investment horizon.
Resources are an issue (capital rationing) and the projects are independent.	Determine if the projects are fractional or not.
Projects are fractional.	Rank by the highest Benefit-Cost Ratio.
Projects are not fractional.	Accept the groupings of projects that yield the highest Net Present Value.
Capital rationing and the projects are mutually exclusive.	Do projects have equal lives?
Projects have equal lives.	Accept the groupings of projects with the highest Net Present Value.
Projects have unequal lives.	Rework the groupings of projects over a common investment horizon.

Conclusion

In conclusion, Chapter 5 discussed how to invest in projects as a whole with an eye on creating value (a macro perspective) for the company. One of the purposes of this chapter was to establish that projects are unique and bear different levels of risk (a micro perspective) than the risk of the company as a whole. In regard to value, it's all about how much cash your company can generate.

The underlying thought is to leverage the cost of a company's money from the owners of the equity and the debt with projects that generate positive returns. In order to establish awareness and recognition of how cash is generated, invested, and reported, a thorough explanation of how a statement of cash flows is constructed was supplied. The statement was further defined as an instrument that provides information about the magnitude and composition of a company's cash generating power.

The three sections of the statement of cash flows were delineated and explained. Those three sections were divided into operating activities, investing activities, and financing activities. The statement of cash flows laid the foundation for the concept of free cash flows. The procedure for deriving free cash flows from the statement of cash flows as well as a shortcut was discussed.

Once the tools for understanding how to derive cash flow were introduced, the concept of capital budgeting was introduced. Capital budgeting is the process of choosing one project over another given the constraints of the company. The projects under consideration must be evaluated. The financial evaluation process consists of three steps: calculating the relevant cash flows, choosing a figure of merit, and establishing acceptance criteria. In calculating the relevant cash flows, five considerations must be taken into account: self-generating working capital, sunk costs, allocated expenses, excess capacity, and financing costs. The figures of merit discussed were:

- Accounting rate of return
- Payback period
- Net present value
- Internal rate of return
- Benefit-cost ratio

The latter three figures of merit take into consideration the time value of money and to some extent adjust for individual project risk. The acceptance criteria of the figures of merit were shown in Exhibit 6.12.

The idea of acceptance criteria was further complicated by real-world problems, such as not enough money to do all of the accepted projects (capital rationing), projects that conflict with one or another (mutually exclusive), and projects of unequal lives. All of the permutations of the combinations of the real-world problems were discussed. In all the permutations except for one, NPV was the safe choice for the figure of merit. The purpose of the financial evaluation is to select the projects that create the most value. The idea is to create value with all of the projects in order to create value for the company as a whole.

Notes

1. Dan Pallais and Stephen D. Holton, *Forecasts and Projects*, (Fort Worth, TX: Practitioners Publishing Company, 2004), 103.13–103.14.

2. Ibid.

3. Robert C. Higgins, *Analysis for Financial Management* (New York: McGraw-Hill, 2004) 248–258.

CHAPTER 7

Creating the Project Budget

Introduction

Consider the statement: Projects do not happen in a vacuum. This certainly is a truism. However, in our previous book, *The Essentials of Strategic Project Management*, we pointed out that many companies consider projects and project management as if they exist in a vacuum.[1] Companies often tell us: "We need project management training." The attitude conveyed by that statement shows that projects and project management are considered to exist in a vacuum.

Any company can improve the manner in which projects are executed to become more efficient. However, no matter how efficient a project team may be, if the project being executed is not in alignment with the company's financial goals and strategy, there is a limit to how the company will profit from the project.

A project's budget must be based on the company's strategy and financial goals. These goals are reflected by the company's budget, which may be represented by a number of different documents, including pro forma or projected revenue and expense, cash flow, and balance sheets. The project budget that is based on the company's financial planning has a much greater chance of contributing to the company's success. In this chapter, we will first look at the process of creating a company's operating budget. Later we will move on to project budgets and how they relate to the company's operating budget.

To create the company's operating budget, we must bring together and synthesize most of the information contained in the previous 6 chapters. In creating an operating budget, financial managers decide how to use company resources to achieve their financial goals. In turn, the financial goals support the company in achieving other goals and objectives according to the company's mission.

Case Study: Pontrelli Recycling, Inc.

Let's return to Pontrelli Recycling, Inc., the company that we first saw as an illustration in Chapter 2. Pontrelli Recycling, Inc.'s mission is twofold:

1. Increase the efficiency of recycling usable materials in order to create a better environment for all
2. Create value and a fair return on investment for shareholders

Let us see how the company's mission statement and financial goals, along with the results of maintaining an agile business, become the basis for financial managers to decide how they will operate the company in the coming year and how that will affect the choice and execution of projects. Please note that some of the information contained in the Pontrelli exhibits in this chapter has been slightly altered to accommodate the case study.

Increasing the efficiency of recycling usable materials implies benefits not only for the environment, but also for Pontrelli Recycling, Inc. Pontrelli has focused on information in its business environment, gathering information on the competition as well as new developments in recycling technology. This research constitutes the Awareness Loop of their Agile systems (see the section on Business Agility in Chapter 3). The research has shown that both municipalities and companies would be interested in using the recycling services of a company that was able to provide two benefits:

1. It could cut the cost of recycling for clients.
2. It could increase the range of recycled materials that could be handled.

When comparing potential customer demand with new developments in recycling equipment the Balance Loop of the Pontrelli Recycling, Inc. Agile process showed that they were presented with several opportunities. First, if the company could decrease the cost of recycling, perhaps it could pass on a part of the savings to clients and also increase its own profitability. Decreasing the cost to clients would make Pontrelli Recycling, Inc. more competitive in the market and could be used to increase its client base and revenues.

Second, if Pontrelli Recycling, Inc. were able to increase the range of materials that it was able to recycle, it would be able to increase the revenue realized from each client by providing more recycling services. Pontrelli Recycling, Inc. would then be in the enviable position of not only increasing revenues through new clients but also increasing revenue from each client.

Once Pontrelli understood the opportunities, they applied the Agility Loop to consider the other side of Pontrelli Recycling, Inc.'s mission statement—to increase value and provide a fair return on shareholder investment. If shareholders were used to seeing a 43 percent increase in their stock value each year, as well as an annual dividend of $1,000, then the company's managers would need to determine whether those financial goals could be met by finding a way of increasing efficiency and recycling more kinds of materials.

In addition, Pontrelli Recycling, Inc. must consider the competition in the marketplace. Not only must the company's leaders decide if it can financially create a benefit by increasing the company's capabilities, it must also see what the risk is if they do not. Just as Pontrelli Recycling, Inc. could potentially increase its base of clients by implementing increased capabilities, it could also lose market share if it does not and the competition does.

On the financial side, we recall that Pontrelli Recycling, Inc. had a return on equity of 43 (43.2 percent), meaning that every dollar of equity (what shareholders own) that was employed produced 43.2 cents of net income. The company also had a return on capital of 29.5 percent; in other words, for every dollar of capital (the goods used to operate the company), 29.5 cents of net income was produced. In addition, the company had a net profit margin of 4.5 percent, indicating that for every dollar of revenue, Pontrelli produced 4.5 cents of net profit. Other information on Pontrelli Recycling, Inc. can be found in Exhibit 2.5 of Chapter 2.

Pontrelli Recycling, Inc.'s financial objectives included increasing the value of the company as well as creating a fair return for shareholders. The company has fulfilled this objective by increasing stock value and paying a dividend. It is difficult for a company to control the value of its stock, which is a reflection of the value that the marketplace places on a company. Essentially, stock price is the market's evaluation of a company's potential to produce earnings in the future. While Pontrelli Recycling, Inc. cannot directly control the price of its stock, it can, in large part, control its ability to produce earnings in the future.

In regard to planning an operational budget for a given year; financial managers must first make decisions about the company's financial and other objectives and then decide how to make those decisions a reality through operations. Managers use information such as the financial ratios to make the decisions and then employ those ratios as they operate the company to see if they are producing the intended results.

If Pontrelli Recycling, Inc.'s management would like to increase value then they must convince the market that they are capable of producing income in the future. There are many factors in producing income, including the company's internal capacities, but there are also external influences, such as the condition of the market and competition. How a company responds to all of the influences will dictate its results. During a strong, expanding economy, the company that does not invest and increase capacity may lose out. During a weak or contracting economy, the company that overestimates its ability to expand may be the loser.

Let's return to Pontrelli Recycling, Inc.'s financial ratios to see how the information can inform decision making. Certainly, profit margin can be improved by decreasing cost or improving efficiency without increasing revenues. If Pontrelli Recycling, Inc. were to decrease its cost of sales by $500,000, for example, it would increase its net profit margin to 5.4 percent and thus improve its return on equity to 50.8 percent. In other words, for every dollar of equity, the company would be producing 50.8 cents of net income. That represents a 14.5 percent increase in return on equity. The marketplace would normally notice such an increase.

Although the marketplace normally notices such an increase, if a competitor of Pontrelli Recycling, Inc.'s announces that it has implemented technology and processes to increase efficiency and widen the number of recyclable products, there could be a negative effect on Pontrelli's stock, despite the company's increased efficiency.

In addition to increasing value, Pontrelli Recycling, Inc. increases its annual dividend to shareholders. That dividend must come from somewhere. If the company increases efficiency and does not increase spending, it probably will also have an increase in cash on hand at the end of the year. One of the ways that Pontrelli Recycling, Inc. could deal with that cash is by giving more of it to the stockholders as a dividend. However, in order to maintain the increased dividend in the future, the gains in efficiency must be enduring, and revenues must also increase year over year.

So, Pontrelli Recycling, Inc. must decide now how to meet its financial objectives. There are a number of ways to do this. We have already discussed increased efficiency to improve profit margin, but there are others. The company could also increase revenues; however, increased revenues without increased efficiency will increase the amount of profits but not the underlying financial ratios. Increased income with the same profit margin will not affect ratios at all.

If Pontrelli Recycling, Inc. wishes to pursue new technology that will allow it to increase efficiency and expand the range of materials that can be recycled, there will without doubt be increased expenditures. Therefore, the company's managers must look at all of the different aspects of the increased spending to try to decide whether to move ahead. On one hand, they must try and predict what effect the investment will have in revenue: for example, how many more clients do they believe that they will be able to acquire over a given time period in order to increase revenue? How much revenue will they be able to predict from existing clients due to additional materials that they will be able to recycle?

On the other hand, expenditures must be made in order to create the new capabilities. Some will be capital expenditures, equipment purchases, and construction of new plants or refurbishing of old plants. Pontrelli Recycling, Inc. may have to purchase new trucks and even provide new containers for clients. Capital expenditures must be amortized over a certain number of years. The manner in which capital expenditures are financed must also be considered. Will they be financed by debt or equity? Managers must review the cost of each and the affect on each of the ratios.

In addition to capital expenditures, there may be other costs to consider. For example, new equipment and processes probably will result in a need for staff training, which is not a cost that can be amortized over a period of years. Increased current costs will affect net profit, so managers must decide if the increased cost will be offset by increased revenues during a time period that will allow them to pay the increased dividends to shareholders.

In order to create an operational budget, managers must look beyond the special project. They must also determine what amounts must be budgeted to provide for operations during the year. These amounts would include operations and any other one-time projects that must be considered. In the example of Pontrelli Recycling, Inc., a significant increase in the number of clients and volume of business could have other ramifications. For example, the company might need to hire more workers to man an increased number of trucks. The decision might include several options: Is it more cost effective to have trucks and workers work overtime to cope with the increase or to purchase additional vehicles and hire new workers?

The addition of more clients and consequently more workers may have other ramifications. Perhaps Pontrelli Recycling, Inc. will need to upgrade its accounting system to process an increase in billing and collections or install a new payroll system to handle the increased number of workers. The new technology may provide new client opportunities. Clients may seek assistance in developing new procedures to handle the increased materials. This could represent new revenue stream as well as new project costs.

Planning for the Future

In the planning process, financial managers look at a series of conjectures in order to determine the company's path for a future time period. Many companies have extended multiple-year plans, but such plans are less detailed than an operating budget and are for guidance toward long-term objectives. What we will view here is a one-year forecast for Pontrelli Recycling, Inc. that will take into consideration decisions that the company will make about operations for the coming year.

Once we have gone through the forecasting process for the entire firm, we will look at the budget process for one of the projects that the decisions require, in order to see how the budget fits into the overall operating budget of the company and how decisions are made as to the viability of the project. We will then look at project execution, to see how the project budget is realized through the execution of the project and how project performance is tracked against the budget.

Pro Forma Statements

As we have seen in Chapter 6, pro forma statements can be used in the budgeting process. In this case, we will start with Pontrelli Recycling, Inc.'s statements as of December 31, 2005, and build future-looking statements. For a reference, we first create a baseline 2006 statement that predicts what business will look like if no changes are made. Next, we create documents that take into account the predicted costs and revenues that might result based on decisions that are made.

Note that there is a difference between the forecast figures that are used when planning at a company-wide level and those that are created for a project. The forecasts are normally created from the top down and represent estimates that are accurate within a certain percentage.

Final project budgets are usually done from the bottom up and represent a more accurate picture of actual expenditures. One of the keys to moving beyond being a project manager to being a financial manager is being able to see and understand the big picture when working on an individual project. This can be one of the most challenging features of project management, whether in a large or small company.

To begin our consideration of how management might approach planning for next year, let's set down a baseline of information. In Exhibit 7.1, we see a pro forma income and expense statement for 2006. Although Pontrelli Recycling, Inc.'s growth rate for 2005 was 13 percent, we are proposing a more modest rate of 5 percent. As you can see, the results of an across-the-board increase of 5 percent to revenue and expenses means a modest rise in net profit.

In addition to a pro forma income and expense statement, the managers would also prepare a pro forma balance sheet (see Exhibit 7.2). Note that the growth rate of 5 percent was not assigned to every line in the balance sheet. Cash, accounts receivable, and inventory were allowed to grow at the same rate as sales, as were taxes payable. However, we are not assuming similar growth rates in long-term assets, debt, or equity. As a result, while total assets and debt plus equity increased by 25 percent, equity by itself actually increased

EXHIBIT 7.1 Income Statement Including Pro Forma 2011

<table>
<tr><td colspan="4" align="center">Pontrelli Recycling Inc.</td></tr>
<tr><td></td><td>2009</td><td>2010</td><td>Pro Forma 2011</td></tr>
<tr><td>Sales</td><td>$32,751,694</td><td>$36,957,183</td><td>$38,805,042</td></tr>
<tr><td>Cost Of Sales</td><td>28,273,539</td><td>31,552,817</td><td>33,130,457</td></tr>
<tr><td>Gross Profit</td><td>4,478,155</td><td>5,404,366</td><td>5,674,584</td></tr>
<tr><td>Selling, Administrative, and General Expenses (Operating Expenses)</td><td>2,541,286</td><td>2,459,287</td><td>2,656,029</td></tr>
<tr><td>Special Projects</td><td></td><td></td><td>500,000</td></tr>
<tr><td>Income From Operations</td><td>1,936,869</td><td>2,945,079</td><td>2,518,554</td></tr>
<tr><td>Interest Expense</td><td>129,398</td><td>142,608</td><td>149,738</td></tr>
<tr><td>Income Before Taxes</td><td>1,807,471</td><td>2,802,471</td><td>3,026,668</td></tr>
<tr><td>Income Taxes</td><td>722,988</td><td>1,120,988</td><td>1,210,667</td></tr>
<tr><td>Dividend</td><td>108,448</td><td>168,148</td><td>181,600</td></tr>
<tr><td>Net Income</td><td>$ 976,034</td><td>$ 1,513,334</td><td>$ 1,634,401</td></tr>
</table>

by 30 percent. This was because there was no corresponding increase in debt to match the increase in assets.

As shown in Exhibit 7.2, the baseline scenario for Pontrelli Recycling, Inc. shows that without any major changes and a modest increase in sales, there will be modest changes in the balance sheet. It would seem that by maintaining the status quo, the company can continue to make modest gains. However, when we look at Pontrelli Recycling, Inc.'s profitability ratios, we see that while profit margins and expense ratios are unchanged, return on equity and return on capital are eroding.

Return on equity is diminishing because equity is increasing more rapidly than income growth. Income is increasing and much of the income is being retained as cash, increasing total assets. Since cash accumulation does not result in a corresponding increase in debt, the increase in total assets is balanced by an increase in equity.

EXHIBIT 7.2 Balance Sheet Including Pro Forma 2011

Pontrelli Recycling, Inc.

December 31	2009	2010	Pro Forma 2011
Cash	$2,254,815	$3,768,150	$5,402,551
Accounts Receivable	564,532	1,645,827	1,728,118
Inventory	1,331,940	1,153,515	1,211,191
Total Current Assets	4,151,287	6,567,492	8,343,866
Net Property, Plant, and Equip.	369,116	214,119	214,119
Other Assets	211,190	188,482	197,906
Less Depreciation			
Total Assets	$4,731,593	$6,970,093	$8,755,891
Accounts Payable	27,246	259,663	272,646
Notes Payable Short Term	425,786	440,318	440,318
Payroll and Sales Tax Payable	1,490	85,374	89,643
State Income Taxes Payable	0	711	768
Total Current Liabilities	454,522	786,066	803,375
Notes Payable Long Term	1,221,905	1,129,228	1,129,228
Total Liabilities	1,676,427	1,915,294	1,932,603
Stockholders' Equity	3,055,166	5,054,799	6,823,288
Total Liabilities	$4,731,593	$6,970,093	$8,755,891

Therefore, each dollar of equity invested is producing less net income (see Exhibit 7.3). Return on capital is diminishing because the excess cash is not generating the return that properly deployed assets are producing.

A short-term solution to readjust the ratio could be to increase the amount of the dividend paid to owners. In the case of cash-rich

EXHIBIT 7.3 2010 Ratios Compared to 2011 Pro Forma

Pontrelli Recycling, Inc.		
	2010	2011
Return on Equity	37.3%	24.7%
Leverage Multiplier	1.44	1.32
Return on Capital	25.87%	18.67%
Net Profit Margin	4.09%	4.21%
Operating Profit Margin	7.97%	6.49%
Gross Profit Margin	14.62%	14.62%
Operating Expense	6.65%	6.84%
Tax Rate	40.00%	40.00%

companies (e.g., Microsoft in the early 2000s), many stockholders feel that dividends are an appropriate way of passing value to the owners and rebalancing return on equity.

It is clear that if Pontrelli Recycling, Inc. accepts the status quo, in a few years time its financial position will erode and will make it harder to attain the company's mission and objectives. The company's financial managers must make decisions about how to operate the company in the future. There are many possible actions that the managers could take to improve performance, but we will concentrate on one example, that is, acquiring new technology in an effort to become more efficient and to be able to recycle more kinds of materials.

In order to plan for the future, Pontrelli Recycling, Inc.'s managers must prepare pro forma documents that will reflect the assumptions that they make concerning future performance. In this case, the assumptions will be based on the company's desire to increase efficiency, increase business from current clients, and expand its client base by acquiring new technology, allowing it to process materials more efficiently and expanding the types of materials that it is able to recycle. The basic assumptions are:

- By acquiring the new technology, Pontrelli Recycling, Inc. will be able to increase sales by 15 percent in 2007, 25 percent in 2008 and 2009, and 20 percent in 2010. The projections are based on performance specifications of the technology and market research and analysis by the marketing department.

- It is expected that, due to the efficiency of the new technology and related processes, increase in the cost of sales (what it costs to run the technology) and selling and general administration cost will rise at a rate less than sales increase and will gradually decrease in relation to the percent rise in sales.
- After five years there will be gradually diminishing increases in sales revenue.
- The cost of the project will be approximately $8 million including $7.5 million for equipment and installation, and $500,000 for project management, process change, and training.
- The $7.5 million for equipment and installation will be financed by a 10-year loan at 8 percent. The $500,000 will be paid cash as a special project line item in the income and expense statement.
- The equipment will be amortized over a 10-year period with equal amounts of 10 percent amortized over 10 years.

First, we review the pro forma income and revenue statement to see what effects the acquisition of technology will create. In Exhibit 7.4, we can see that on the top line, revenues have increased by almost 100 percent between 2006 and 2010, while net income is up 600 percent over the same period. The effect of the increase in sales would be magnified by the increased efficiency and the fact that the new technology would allow for decreasing costs in cost of sales and sales and general administration.

An increase in efficiency that enables workers to be more productive decreases expenses because the rate of hiring new employees would be lower than the rate of increasing sales. In addition, hiring fewer new employees would save the company money on training as well as general administration costs.

Note that the situation described in the income and expense statement shows that the move would generate a large amount of cash; so

EXHIBIT 7.4 Pro Forma Income and Expense

Pontrelli Recycling Inc. Pro Forma Income and Expense for the Year Ending

	2011	2012	2013	2014	2015
Sales	$38,805,042	$42,685,546	$51,222,655	$61,467,186	$70,687,264
Cost of Sales	33,130,457	34,786,980	40,005,027	46,005,782	48,306,071
Gross Profit	5,674,584	7,898,565	11,217,627	15,461,404	22,381,193
Selling, Administrative, and General Expenses					
(Operating Expenses)	2,656,029	2,921,632	3,213,796	3,535,175	3,711,934
Special Projects	500,000				
Income from Operations	2,518,554	4,976,933	8,003,832	11,926,229	18,669,259
Interest Expense	$ 149,738	$ 892,608	$ 892,608	$ 892,608	$ 892,608
Income before Taxes	3,026,668	4,084,324	7,111,223	11,033,620	17,776,650
Income Taxes	1,210,667	1,633,729	2,844,489	4,413,448	7,110,660
Dividend	181,600	245,059	853,346	1,324,034	2,133,198
Net Income	$ 1,634,401	$ 2,205,535	$ 3,413,387	$ 5,296,138	$ 8,532,792

153

much so that in 2008, the rate of dividend would be doubled to 20 percent. Despite the dividend increase, Pontrelli Recycling, Inc. would continue to generate large amounts of cash.

Let us now turn to Pontrelli Recycling, Inc.'s pro forma balance sheet (Exhibit 7.5). The first significant change here is in assets. The purchase of new equipment valued at $7.5 million has caused a dramatic increase in property, plant, and equipment to over $7.7 million, bringing total assets to over $17.5 million. Property, plant, and equipment have been depreciated during the first year at a rate of 10 percent and have been subtracted from total assets.

The $7.5 million increase noted in property, plant, and equipment is balanced by an increase of the same amount in notes payable long term. As a result, stockholder's equity has also increased by the difference between total assets and total liabilities.

If we follow stockholder's equity from 2006 to 2010, we see three-fold increase over that time. There are two reasons why equity increased to such a great degree. First, notes payable long term gradually decreases over that time. Second, while current liabilities increase, they do not increase at anywhere near the rate that cash does. Since cost of sales and sales and general administration are taking a decreasing percentage of sales, cash will increase. As total assets increase due to cash and total liabilities decreases due to debt payments, stockholder's equity must increase. Chances are the company's stock value will increase as well.

Now let's turn to Pontrelli's profitability ratios (Exhibit 7.6). Note that for 2006, the year before the project will take effect, return on equity and return on capital decrease. Return on equity decreased because equity grew faster than income during 2006, as did capital in relation to income. Income slowed because Pontrelli Recycling, Inc. is not acquiring new clients at the same rate as previously and is not expanding sales as quickly as before. The company's management must look at alternatives, as the status quo is slow stagnation.

As we view the pro forma portion of the ratios, we can see that all of the ratios gradually begin to improve and by 2010 are for the most

EXHIBIT 7.5 Pontrelli Recycling, Inc.'s Pro Forma Balance Sheet

Pontrelli Recycling Inc. Pro Forma Balance Sheet For Year Ending

	2011	2012	2013	2014	2015
Cash	$ 5,402,551	$ 7,608,086	$ 11,021,473	$ 16,317,611	$ 24,850,404
Accounts Receivable	1,728,118	1,814,524	1,905,250	2,000,513	2,100,539
Inventory	1,211,191	1,271,750	1,335,338	1,402,105	1,472,210
Total Current Assets	8,343,866	10,694,361	14,262,062	19,720,229	28,423,152
Net Property, Plant, and Equip.	214,119	7,714,119	7,714,119	7,714,119	7,714,119
Other Assets	197,906	217,697	239,466	275,386	316,694
Less Depreciation	0	1,102,016	2,201,949	3,301,882	4,401,815
Total Assets	$ 8,755,891	$ 17,524,160	$ 20,013,698	$ 24,407,852	$ 32,052,151
Accounts Payable	272,646	299,911	329,902	379,387	436,295
Notes Payable Short Term	440,318	462,334	485,451	509,723	535,209
Payroll and Sales Tax Payable	89,643	120,968	187,216	290,480	468,002
State Income Taxes Payable	768	845	929	1,069	1,229
Total Current Liabilities	803,375	884,057	1,003,497	2,690,929	5,381,858
Notes Payable Long Term	1,129,228	8,629,228	7,766,305	6,989,675	6,290,707
Total Liabilities	1,932,603	9,513,285	8,769,802	9,680,604	11,672,565
Stockholders' Equity	6,823,288	8,010,875	11,243,896	14,727,249	20,379,585
Total Liabilities and Stockholders' Equity	$ 8,755,891	$ 17,524,160	$ 20,013,698	$ 24,407,852	$ 32,052,151

EXHIBIT 7.6 Pro Forma Profitability Ratios

Pontrelli Recycling, Inc. Profitability Ratios						
	2010	2011	2012	2013	2014	2015
ROE	37.3%	24.7%	27.5%	30.4%	39.3%	46.49%
Leverage	1.44	1.32	1.77	1.95	1.80	1.77
ROC	25.87%	18.67%	12.59%	17.06%	21.70%	26.62%
NPM	4.09%	4.21%	5.17%	6.66%	8.62%	12.07%
OPM	7.97%	6.49%	11.66%	15.63%	19.40%	26.41%
GPM	14.62%	14.62%	22.71%	28.04%	33.61%	46.33%
OER	6.65%	6.84%	6.84%	6.27%	5.75%	5.25%

part significantly improved over 2006. This effect is being caused by several factors: first, increased sales are fueling company growth at a greater rate than previously experienced. Second, greater efficiency decreases the rate of growth in both cost of sales and in sales and general administration, thus improving profitability and increasing cash flow.

In addition, the increased cash flow is permitting Pontrelli Recycling, Inc. to reduce long-term debt in a timely fashion while also fueling an increase in cash reserves. The decreased liabilities and increased cash fuel growth in both capital and equity, therefore improving all of the other profitable ratios.

Now, if all pro forma statements were an accurate picture of the future, most companies would never suffer any financial woes. We all know that the real world is often more unpredictable than a rosy spreadsheet. Therefore, Pontrelli Recycling, Inc.'s management would be wise to create other pro forma statements that would reflect more conservative growth rates, greater expenses, and other problems that could occur.

Managers should also look at the likelihood of a competitor implementing the same technology at the same time as Pontrelli Recycling, Inc. did. For the sake of illustration, let's say that Pontrelli Recycling, Inc. reviewed its alternatives and felt that the pro forma statement shown in Exhibit 7.5 was actually the most likely scenario. The company must take two other steps in creating a budget.

First, the managers must make decisions about how company assets will be allocated to operations in the coming year. They must decide on operating budgets for each area or department of the company. For example, they would need to decide what amounts of money must be allocated within cost of sales to generate the predicted revenue stream. This cost includes salaries and benefits for production employees. It may also include operating costs for vehicles and equipment, such as gas and electricity, permits and licenses, and other costs.

Second, after managers determine these costs at a high level, they normally pass the detailed budget on to management in each department for review and confirmation. The senior managers would estimate whether they would be able to operate the department effectively within that budget. Each department would now develop its detailed budget based on the information received from management. The mechanics of budget development within a department is not our focus in this book, so we will not go into more detail.

A critical project is also being planned for Pontrelli Recycling, Inc. So far, estimates of the cost of the project are top-down. These are accurate to a point, but due diligence requires that the company create a more detailed project budget to confirm the predicted costs and to review the project more closely for risk and opportunity.

Creating a Project Budget

In our previous work, *The Essentials of Strategic Project Management*, we covered in great detail the process of initiating and planning projects. We will review the first two phases of project management briefly here and cover only the development of the project budget in detail.

During project initiation, the project charter is created, which contains crucial information about the project, including client goals and objectives, specific project goals, and information about various stakeholders. Most important, the project charter describes the project's high-level deliverables. It also describes project success, what it is and how it will be measured.

During project planning, the project team starts with the high-level deliverables and creates a work breakdown structure that describes the detailed work tasks that must be completed. A project schedule is then created, linking the work tasks in their proper order and showing what must be done when. Next, resources are defined for the project, both people and materials. Once this has been done, the project team has a great deal of information about the project:

- Detailed deliverables with notations as to what they are and what they do
- A set of tasks that describe the work necessary to complete the deliverables
- A list of resources needs to complete the tasks, including personnel and other resources
- Estimates of the effort needed from the resources to complete the tasks
- A list of constraints about resources needed, including availability, and the need for training
- A schedule of when each task will start and be completed, giving rise to the finish date

All of this information becomes input into the budget process. As we develop the project budget, we will use information from Chapter 4, such as determining project cash flows, to determine the breakdown of costs as well as timing of costs and expenditures. When we are finished, we will be able to compare this bottom-up approach to creating a project budget with the top-down project budget created earlier. Finally we want to reconcile the two budgets to ensure that they are both accurate. The information gathered during reconciliation should play a crucial role in the final decision about the project.

It is not unusual for a company to complete project initiation before making a decision about a large, important project such as the one Pontrelli Recycling, Inc. is considering.

As mentioned, the high-level cost estimate of the project is $8 million, with $7.5 million coming from a long-term note and $.5 million from cash flow. We can break these numbers down into a fairly simple budget. Using the work breakdown structure (Exhibit 7.7), we get a picture of the work that must be completed. While the work breakdown structure could certainly be decomposed farther, this will serve our purposes.

The main project activities will involve preparing the plant for new equipment and include renovating and expanding the existing plant and acquiring and installing the equipment. From the operations side, existing processes must be reviewed and updated. When the work breakdown structure is completed, all of the work that must be performed in order to complete the project has been identified.

Once the detailed information on what work must be done is complete, the project team will create the network diagram, illustrating the order in which the work must be completed, and determine the people needed to complete the work and when they will be needed. They will also determine the cost of any materials needed—the largest part of this project. At this point the project team will be able to create the project budget based on the detailed project plan as well as a cash flow table illustrating the timing of cash outflows and finance needs.

The project estimate in Exhibit 7.8 is about 6 percent more than the budget estimate.

There is a caveat: In order to maintain the same cost for new equipment and trucks, Pontrelli Recycling, Inc. must commit to the purchase within 90 days. In addition, the project estimate includes risk contingency of 12 percent of the cost of the project. When adding the estimate difference and the risk cost into the company's financial statements, the additional cost did not create a significant effect on those financials.

EXHIBIT 7.7 Work Breakdown Structure

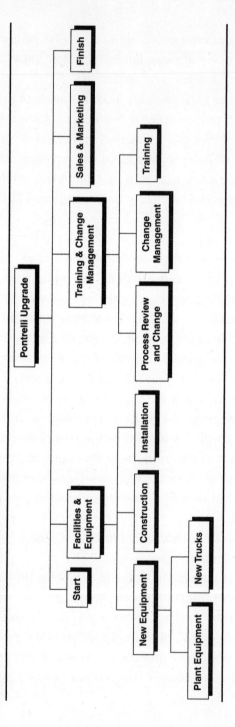

EXHIBIT 7.8 Project Budget

Detailed Estimates	Budget	Project
Project Initiation and Planning	100,000	110,000
Plant Equipment	5,000,000	5,000,000
New Trucks	750,000	750,000
Construction	800,000	1,016,000
Installation	450,000	495,000
Process Review and Change	150,000	162,000
Project Management	125,000	127,500
Training	125,000	130,000
	7,500,000	7,790,500
Totals	**Budget Estimate**	**Project Estimate**
Equipment	5,750,000	5,750,000
Construction and Renovation	1,250,000	1,511,000
Training and Change Management	500,000	529,500
	7,500,000	7,790,500
Percentage Difference		**5.80%**

Review Project Financials

According to Pontrelli Recycling, Inc.'s pro forma financial statement, it appears that the technology acquisition project will be profitable for the company. Before the company makes a final decision, it must also consider the actual cost of the project as compared to the additional revenue that will flow into the company as a result of the project.

If we do a comparison of net income between a baseline (continued 5 percent growth over 10 years) and the assumptions provided by this project, we can see that there is significant added revenue with the project. However, Pontrelli Recycling, Inc. needs to determine whether this added revenue is worth more to the company than not doing the project and continuing with the baseline revenue calculations.

In Exhibit 7.9 we can see that the cumulative value of projected baseline revenues over a 10-year period is $16,686,882, assuming that revenues continue to grow at 5 percent annually and Pontrelli

EXHIBIT 7.9 Projected Income

Total Net Income 2009–2016		
	Net Income	NPV
Baseline (5%)	$16,686,882	$ 8,534,627
Project	$51,988,253	$40,052,357
Additional Net Income		$31,517,729
IRR		30.64%

Recycling, Inc. maintains market share. We can also see that according to the pro forma income estimates, if the project is undertaken, the cumulative revenues would be $51,988,253, a significant difference.

As mentioned in Chapter 6, net present value (NPV) represents the value today of future cash flows. If we compare the NPV of the projected baseline revenues with that of the project's projected revenues, we see a difference of over $31 million. The internal rate of return (IRR), the rate of return at which the project returns no profit, is 30.64 percent. Therefore, the cost rate of the project must be less than the IRR. Pontrelli Recycling's weighted average cost of capital is 17.46 percent, significantly below the IRR.

It is quite likely that the company's financial managers would review other scenarios for this work; in particular, they would see what would happen if revenues turned out to be significantly less than what are proposed. Once they feel that they have a realistic case for moving forward, they could begin to execute the work.

Project Cash Flow

Part of financial planning for projects is understanding the inflows and outflows of cash that will be created by the project. A cash flow table is the tool that is used to study such cash flows by breaking inflows and outflows down, usually on a monthly basis. The cash flow table also serves as an important tracking tool, creating a baseline against which project spending can be compared (see Exhibit 7.10).

EXHIBIT 7.10 Cash Flow Table

Pontrelli Project Cash Flow

Project Expenses	Sep-09	Oct-09	Nov-09	Dec-09	Jan-10	Feb-10	Mar-10	Apr-10	May-10	Jun-10	Jul-10	Aug-10	Sep-10
Project Initiation and Planning	50,000	40,000											
Plant Equipment	1,250,000				1,250,000			1,250,000					1,250,000
New Trucks	187,500				187,500			187,500					187,500
Construction	85,000	90,000	92,000	80,000	80,000	95,000	100,000	75,000	35,000	35,000	25,000		
Installation									112,500	112,500	112,500	112,500	
Process Review and Change	18,000	16,500	15,000	15,000	9,000	9,000	1,000	1,000	12,000	15,000	15,000	9,000	8,000
Project Management	15,000	13,750	12,500	12,500	7,500	7,500	7,500	7,500	7,500	7,500	7,500	7,500	7,500
Training	15,000									25,000	25,000	25,000	30,000
Monthly Total	1,620,500	160,250	119,500	107,500	1,534,000	111,500	108,500	1,521,000	167,000	195,000	185,000	154,000	1,483,000

Project Cash Flow	Sep-09	Oct-09	Nov-09	Dec-09	Jan-10	Feb-10	Mar-10	Apr-10	May-10	Jun-10	Jul-10	Aug-10	Sep-10
Cash	98,000	70,250	27,500	27,500	16,500	16,500	8,500	8,500	19,500	47,500	47,500	41,500	45,500
Debt	1,522,500	90,000	92,000	80,000	1,517,500	95,000	100,000	1,512,500	147,500	147,500	137,500	112,500	1,437,500
Total	1,620,500	160,250	119,500	107,500	1,534,000	111,500	108,500	1,521,000	167,000	195,000	185,000	154,000	1,483,000

As we can see in the table, the four months when payments are due on the equipment to be delivered are September 2006 and January, April, and September 2007. At each of these points, the company furnishing the equipment and trucks for the project requires a 25 percent payment. The last payment is made after the equipment is up and running in the recycling center. At times it can be easier to interpret this information with a graph, as shown in Exhibit 7.11. Since this project is being financed mostly with debt, the financial

EXHIBIT 7.11 Cash Flow Table in Graph Format

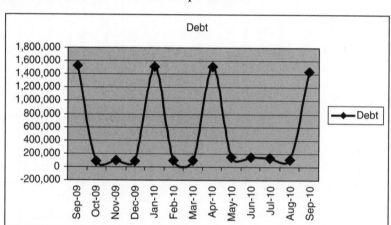

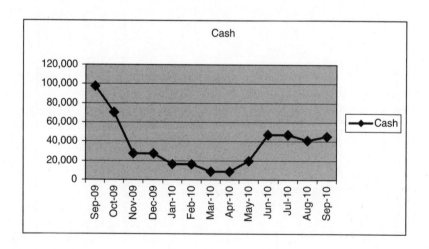

manager of Pontrelli Recycling, Inc. must ensure that the financing is in place at the proper time. In a case like this, many financial institutions arrange for a line of credit that is drawn down over a period of time and then converted to a long-term debt instrument at the completion of the project.

If a substantial portion of this project were being funded with cash, the company's financial managers would also need to compare the project cash flow table with the company's pro forma of overall cash flow, to ensure that there is sufficient cash on hand, in particular during the four months when payment is due for the equipment and trucks. Good project managers always try to ensure that there is good communication between their team and management to avoid any finance problems that could delay the project.

Of course, creating a sound project budget does not guarantee project success. Project information must be gathered in an accurate and timely manner in order to understand what is happening to the project. Financial information is an important part of status reporting, but often it is not even collected. For example, a project where task completion is tracked, but the number of hours actually spent completing tasks is not, may lack the information necessary to know if the project is financially sound.

In the case of an internal project, companies make the mistake of not considering employee time as a real project cost; they must be paid anyway. Although that may be true, in our discussion of cost, we spoke about opportunity cost, that is, the cost of choosing one opportunity over another. If you are not tracking hours worked on a project in an efficient manner, you will not know the real cost of completing a project. It could turn out that due to untracked hours over what was planned, the project is actually costing the company more than originally planned, and another option would have been a better choice.

When the project is for a client, work overruns can quickly eat up a project's profitability. In a fixed price project, adhering to a strict budget is the only way to be profitable. But even in a project that is charging rates, a client may balk at paying significant work overages, leaving the company holding the bag.

The project cash flow statement is a useful tool to understanding how a project is doing financially, but it is important to analyze the information that you are receiving carefully in order to understand what is really happening (see Exhibit 7.10).

Let us suppose that it is the end of December 2006. At this point in the project, the total cash flow for project expenses should be $2,007,750. However, the total expenditure to date is only $1,826,075. At first glance, it looks like the project is coming in slightly under cost. However, a closer look at the costs will reveal something quite different.

Of the budgeted amount, most has gone to the purchase of equipment, $1,250,000 to be exact. Other costs, for the most part construction, are actually $205,575, or about 53 percent of the budget allocated. Since most of these costs are construction related that seems like good news. However, when we review earned value information, we find out that the news is not good.

First of all, compared with the project schedule, the earned value is actually $195,000 and the cost performance index (CPI) is 50 percent. In other words, not only is the project behind schedule, it is seriously over for construction cost. The CPI of 50 percent means that the project is delivering only about 50 cents of value on a dollar spent. When we apply the estimate at completion formula, we find that if the situation is not corrected, construction costs will actually be around $1,572,831 instead of the budgeted $1,016,000, representing a cost overrun of almost 64 percent on construction and 15 percent on the project overall.

A project that is running over cost at 15 percent is a problem, but we don't know if other problems will arise due to the delays, thereby adding to the mounting project cost. In addition, we must consider cash flow. Since the project is being financed 93 percent by debt, cost overruns mean additional borrowing must be made, increasing the cost of interest to the company. Although the amount of the cost overruns at this stage of the project seems small, proper analysis and correction now can prevent greater problems later.

The company must now ensure that it can guarantee additional financing to complete the project. The total cost overrun would lower the projected net income of the project, which in turn lowers NPV of the project by over $800,000. The IRR on the project changed to 27.15 percent, not an insignificant change (see Exhibit 7.12). Fortunately for Pontrelli Recycling, Inc., the change in NPV and IRR is not large enough to cause a serious problem, but it does make the company aware that it must monitor the situation carefully in order to avoid more serious problems. Additional budget overruns in other areas of the project could have serious consequences.

We must also view the effect of such a project overrun on company financials. In Exhibits 7.12 and 7.13, we can see that such a serious cost overrun will have an effect on the financial performance in 2007, as compared to the original estimates in Exhibits 7.6 and 7.9.

EXHIBIT 7.12 Effects of Cost Overrun

	Budget	Actual	Construction Cost Earned Value	
September	$1,620,500	$1,620,500	**Planned Value**	$ 387,250
October	$ 160,250	$ 80,125	**Earned Value**	$ 195,000
November	$ 119,500	$ 71,700	**CPI**	50.36%
December	$ 107,500	$ 53,750	**Estimate at**	
			Completion	$1,572,831
Total	$2,007,750	$1,826,075		

Total Net Income 2011–2018

	Net Income	NPV
Baseline (5%)	$16,686,882	$ 8,534,627
Project	$48,842,772	$39,239,538
Additional Net Income		$30,704,910
IRR		27.00%

EXHIBIT 7.13   Effect of Project Overrun on Financials

	2012*	2012
ROE	18.81%	27.53%
ROC	8.13%	12.59%
NPM	3.18%	5.17%
OPM	7.97%	11.66%

*With Project Overrun

There are significant reductions in return on equity, return on capital, net profit margin, and operating profit margin during the year.

It is clear that inattention to what is happening in a major project can have a serious impact on the company's overall financial performance. What is often ignored, however, is the cumulative effect of many smaller projects. Not every company has major capital projects happening all the time, but many, in particular service companies, have many small projects. Similar problems in many small projects can easily have the same cumulative effect on the financial performance of the company.

Conclusion

As we have seen throughout this chapter, a project's budget does not exist in isolation from the rest of the company. The current financial situation of a company as well as projections into the future must be considered during all phases of the project. When choosing a project, the project manager must take care that it is in alignment with the company's strategic and financial goals and contributes to the growth of the company.

Senior project managers who would like to continue to add value to the company must be able to understand more than the internal functioning of their project. They must also be able to understand the larger picture of the company and how their project fits into and affects that picture. Fortunately, the problems identified in the Pontrelli Recycling, Inc. example, although serious and having a significant effect on the future financial picture, were not so great that the project should be canceled. However, if project managers did not have the larger financial picture, they would not be able to advise the company on possible outcomes.

Note

1. Kevin Callahan and Lynne Brooks, *The Essentials of Strategic Project Management* (Hoboken, NJ: John Wiley & Sons, 2004).

CHAPTER 8

Risk Assessment

Risk assessment has long been a tool in the project manager's arsenal, and there are many books, articles, and Internet commentaries on the topic. Since this book is taking a different angle in its view of project management, we will look at risk assessment from a different point of view—accounting and auditing practices. The primary focus of this chapter is in identifying those risks that would concern an auditor or accounting professional. We believe that this additional knowledge, as well as traditional risk assessment as practiced by project management professionals, will improve your overall skills. In addition, the tools and techniques provided in this chapter will help you assess the risk in being employed by a company and be useful during an employment search as well as leading up to a contract project management engagement.

The *New Oxford American Dictionary* defines risk as "the possibility that something unpleasant or unwelcome will happen." Risk assessment has become more popular in current times because of the meltdown of the financial credit markets in 2008. In fact, the insurance and auditing professions have been aware of the concept since the beginning of their respective industries. In the insurance industry, risk assessment is used in the formulation of customer acceptance and premium calculation. The audit profession relies heavily on the use of risk assessment when an auditor is designing procedures and audit programs. The audit profession essentially breaks down the process into five general steps.

These five steps are an iterative process because the findings or conclusions in a step might cause one to redo a prior step. The five general steps are to:

1. Perform risk assessment procedures.
2. Obtain an understanding of an entity and its environment.
3. Understand the internal controls.
4. Understand the type of accounting transactions.
5. Assess the operating effectiveness of the entity.

It is clear that the objective of the auditor and the project manager are different. However, risk assessment for project management will be going through the same essential steps. The objective will focus on the risk associated with accepting a particular engagement and the risk of a project being knocked off its course.

Wikipedia defines risk assessment as "the determination of quantitative or qualitative value of risk related to a concrete situation and a recognized threat (also called a hazard)." Risk assessment is about studying the impact and the effect of all potential known risks on a project and the alternative actions that can be taken should that risk arise. When quantifying risk for purposes of risk assessment there are two dimensions of calculations. One must calculate the magnitude of a potential loss and the probability that the loss will occur. In order to perform these calculations, you will need to base them on assumptions and uncertainties. By definition, assumptions and uncertainties are very difficult to measure.

Those of you who obtained degrees in business, accounting, and finance should have had the pleasure of taking at least one class on Statistical Analysis or "Statistics". Here lies one of the many reasons why that class was important. According to Professor David Hartvigsen of the University of Notre Dame, "Statistics is the study of collecting, analyzing, presenting, and interpreting data". In general the study of Statistics includes, but is not limited to, descriptive statistics, probability and distributions, hypothesis testing, quality control, and regression.

Descriptive statistics is a set of data that is summarized in an easily understood format. An example of descriptive statistics would be the average annual income of a family living in New York's five boroughs—Manhattan, Bronx, Brooklyn, Queens, and Staten Island.

Probability and distributions begin with collecting and graphing data that has been gathered. Once a graph has been constructed a mean, or average, is calculated and plotted on the graph. The plotting of *Normal Distributions* of data creates a curve that resembles a bell. A bell curve will help you predict what percentage of values will fall within a certain range from the mean, as well as to understand when you have outliers. Outliers are pieces of data that may seem out of place compared to the set of data being analyzed. At the risk of over simplification, there are formulas for estimating the probability of a certain piece of data falling within a certain distance to the mean of all the data.

An example of how you could use the concept of a bell curve to reduce risk and improve performance comes from Pontrelli Recycling. After the project to upgrade equipment and process at the recycling plant, Pontrelli needed to estimate to what extent the materials that they are recycling are contaminated, that is, containing materials that they did not want to recycle. The level of contamination would require changes in setting and process to balance efficiency with the safety of the equipment.

Over the first several months after the new equipment was installed, they tracked contamination in each load that was recycled. The results are contained in the bell curve in Exhibit 8.1

EXHIBIT 8.1 Bell Curve

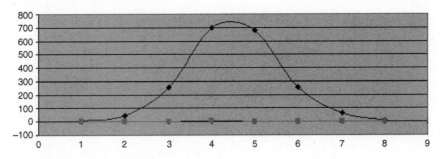

Over the course of 800 lots processed, Pontrelli discovered that contamination ranged from below 1 percent up to 9 percent in some cases, as seen in the X-axis of Exhibit 8.1. The plot in the Y-axis contains the classic bell curve, containing markers for one, two, and three standard deviations, as indicated by the diamonds on the bell curve. According to the rules governing this type of graph, data values will fall along the curve in this way:

- 68 percent of data values within one standard deviation
- 95 percent of data values will fall within two standard deviations
- Nearly 100 percent of values will fall within three standard deviations

Pontrelli can now use that information to decide on settings for their equipment. In Exhibit 8.1, 68 percent of all lots fall between roughly 4 percent and 5 percent contamination and 95 percent of all lots fall between 3 percent and 6 percent contamination. Using this information, Pontrelli can now set their equipment at the percentage of contamination that balances efficiency with safety.

Another type of statistical analysis is hypothesis testing; a process where you test the contradiction of what you expect. An example of this would be that if you expected a light bulb to burn out after 1,000 hours of use, then you would test to see if the light bulbs would burn out with less than 1,000 hours of use. In regard to quality control, samples are taken over time and calculations are done to predict the probability of defects over a certain amount of product produced.

Regression analysis is the process of comparing the relationship between dependent and independent variables. The purpose of this analysis is to be able to predict an outcome based upon a dependent variable. An example of this would be using sales as the dependent variable and advertising costs as the independent variable. Regression analysis could be used to predict anticipated sales given the amount of dollars spent on advertising.

All of these techniques that have been developed under the body of statistics can be easily performed with Microsoft Excel. It is important to note that reliable data must be used and there are a number of ways a mistake can occur or results can be incorrectly interpreted. The correct application of statistics in performing risk assessment is beyond the scope of this chapter. However, be mindful that the use of statistics can assist you in making better decisions. This chapter will focus more on the qualitative decisions about risk assessment.

Risk assessment should be performed to determine whether or not to accept an engagement with an outside contractor, or to initiate a project within a company. The information gathered in the acceptance process should be well documented and revisited while planning for the specific project that you are managing. Given the competition for project management and the scarcity of work, it is almost counter intuitive to think that an outside contractor might recommend declining to take on an engagement. Obviously and ultimately it will be your decision. For an internal project manager, it is often difficult to help a company see from the inside why a project might be too risky. The ensuing questions and procedures are to create a deliberate consciousness in your decision making to proceed with a project or not.

However, if you are an employee project manager, proper risk analysis will help you advise the company on whether or not to move forward with the project. As all of us who have worked as employee project managers know, companies will often move forward with a project despite what a risk analysis reveals. This should not stop you from doing risk analysis!

Risk to Your Reputation

Someone once said "it takes a lifetime to build a good reputation and only a few moments to destroy it". With this in mind, the objective here is to preserve your reputation. Project managers are essentially consultants, even when they are direct employees of a company. Project managers transfer their acquired knowledge and experience to the application of accomplishing a goal, in this case for the purpose of successfully completing a project. In the end it will be about you interacting with many different people. The expectations of those who hire you and of those who have to interact with you will determine whether or not you will get hired and successfully meet your objectives, respectively. Accordingly, your reputation will precede you. It is also important to not lose sight of the fact that in the process of consulting you are giving time out of your life to a project. The waste of that time is no trivial matter.

Competency

When approaching a project as an outside contractor, we recommend that you identify all of your potential client's businesses and product lines, services, and functions. Be sure to understand what the significant business units, departments, and products are. In addition, identify any activities or compliance issues that your potential client may be subject to. For public companies and many non-public companies, this information is readily available on their web sites. For those who don't have informative web sites, we recommend that you call ahead for brochures and do some investigation on the Internet.

The purpose for this analysis is three fold. First, it prepares you for the initial meetings with the potential client. It enhances your ability to understand where the potential client is coming from and heading to. In addition, it allows you to have a better dialogue about the potential engagement with the client. Second, your knowledge about who the client is and what is important to the client should complement the design of your project management. Finally, you should be able to get a feel for whether you have enough experience or knowledge to successfully manage your client's project.

After understanding the client and what is required, you have to prepare an honest self assessment as to whether or not you possess the minimum skills to complete the project. It is important to note that client satisfaction is based upon their expectations of you. Accordingly, managing your clients expectations should be paramount. You do not want to promise your client a Rolls Royce Phantom and in the end deliver a scooter. Do not promise to deliver something that you are unsure of accomplishing. You have to keep in mind that you are being hired to supply expertise that your client is in need of. Failing to meet your client's minimum expectations will probably make for an unpleasant experience for both of you and negatively impact your reputation.

Integrity and Honesty

In addition to assuring yourself that you possess the minimum skill sets to manage a particular project, you need to protect your reputation by knowing whom you are going to be associated with. Your parents warned you as children that you will be defined by the type of friends that you associated with. The old adage comes to mind, "if you lie down with dogs, then you will wake up with fleas". Accordingly, we believe it is important to understand the character of the organization before committing your time and energy to a project. If you are an employee, chances are you did this type of research before being hired by the company.

We recommend that you try to get a feel for your potential client's business ethics. Father Oliver F. Williams, C.S.C., of the University of Notre Dame defined business ethics as "A study of moral standards and how these apply to the system and organization through which modern societies produce and distribute goods and services and to the people who work within these organizations." In order to get a feel for whether or not a potential client has sound business ethics, we recommend that you verify their record. Specifically, we recommend contact with the Better Business Bureau, Chamber of

Commerce, Dun and Bradstreet, and a search for legal complaints. The search for legal complaints and judgments can be accomplished at a relatively low cost by your attorney's office or by subscribing to one of the legal search service providers. A history or pattern of customer, vendor, employee, and/or shareholder complaints should be a red flag ("Caveat Emptor/buyer beware").

The purpose of this analysis in regard to your client's reputation is not to pass judgment as to whether or not you should accept the engagement but to become consciously aware of whom you are working with. If you decide to work for an entity that has exhibited less than honorable behavior, then you should protect yourself accordingly. Be mindful of your reputation and the concept of "guilt by association". Again, if you are an employee of a company, these processes could be useful in your research prior to being hired.

Organizational Structure

The organizational structure of your potential client is telling with regard to what it reveals about business ethics as well. You need to focus on whether or not authority, duties, and responsibilities are properly defined within the organizational structure. From a design perspective, you need to determine whether or not information can travel freely through the organization and whether or not this occurs at all levels, is distributed in a timely fashion, and is accurate (see Exhibit 1.1, The STO Model). It is important to note that you are trying to determine whether an organization is designed to operate openly and transparently, not whether it does. In all likelihood, you will not be able to determine if the company operates as designed until you are engaged. After you gain familiarity do not be surprised to learn that there's a formal organizational structure on paper and in reality a slightly different one. When assessing the organizational structure you need to be mindful about the size and complexity of the organization.

At the risk of stating the obvious, the larger and more complex your client is the more important an open and transparent organizational structure. In addition to the characteristics of organizational structure, you should get a sense of whether or not management demonstrates character, integrity, and ethical values. These characteristics are reflected in management's attitudes, awareness, actions, philosophies, and operating styles. Your potential client's mission and vision statements should be reflected as well. Much of this analysis is subjective and your conclusions will be heavily influenced by your own values.

There are three points to be made here. First, it is important to note that if a company isn't designed to operate openly and transparently, then that doesn't mean it has bad business ethics, but it increases the likelihood of being unpleasantly surprised. Secondly, if your potential client has not gone through the process of defining and designing a sound organizational structure and values, then your potential client will be prone to make bad decisions in times of crisis. Third, if the lines for communication and protocols aren't defined, then your ability to communicate through the organization will be impeded. Plan accordingly.

Human Resources

While examining your potential client's organizational structure be sure to drill a little more deeply into their human resource policies. The signs of a good organization include the communication of messages to employees regarding expected levels of integrity, ethical behavior, and competency. You should determine if the organization is committed to competency. Here are some signs to look for:

- Are there defined minimum skill requirements for each particular job?
- Do they have training and educational programs for professional development and quality assurance?

- Do they ensure that the essential skill sets are provided to each function?
- Do they provide for redundancy and depth in their labor plan?

Reports on Financial Statements

Another area that may be an indicator of your potential client's integrity and financial sustainability is the type of Auditor's Report that is attached to their financial statements. At the risk of over simplification, there are three classes of letters attached to a set of financial statements. They are:

1. Independent Auditors' Report
2. Independent Accountants' Review Report
3. (Independent) Accountants' Compilation Report

The different classes of accountant letters are indicative of the level of assurance on the respective company's financial statements that an independent certified public accounting firm stipulates. In other words the type of letter indicates how much work the accounting firm did relative to proving the accuracy of the financial statements presented.

The "Independent Auditors' Report" is the highest level of assurance and the "(Independent) Accountants' Compilation Report" is the lowest. There is specific and sometimes significant work that needs to be performed by the independent certified public accountants before rendering one of the aforementioned letters. The Independent Auditors' Report, Independent Accountants' Review Report, and (Independent) Accountants' Compilation Report are also referred to as an audit, a review, and a compilation, respectively. The higher the level of assurance by the auditor indicates the greater amount of work performed. The greater the amount of work required is directly proportionate to the cost. For a small company the cost to do an audit is approximately ten times the cost to prepare a compilation. The cost to perform a review is about half the cost of an audit.

The larger the entity the greater the increase in the multiple of costs relative between the three classes of letters. It is also important to note that if an accounting firm performs an audit, review, or compilation for an entity on identical reporting periods, then the accounting firm must issue the report with the highest level of assurance. All publicly traded companies (i.e., those traded on the NYSE or NASDAQ) must have annual audited financial statements or face being delisted from their respective stock exchanges. In many circumstances, lenders require their customers to have their financials prepared at one of the three levels and often require interim financials prepared at a certain level as a covenant of the loan or mortgage documents.

Many foundations require non-profit organizations seeking support to have audited financial statements. In addition, entities seeking government funding are required to have an audit performed on their financials. Independent certified public accounting firms rank as one of the most trusted professions in our society. As a result of this public trust and the plethora of regulations and guidelines, an audited financial statement is accepted as presented.

Earlier we mentioned that there were three classes of letters attached to financial statements. As indicated, the audit is the highest level of assurance, the review is second best, and the compilation is the least. Within those individual classes there is a hierarchy as well. We will not go through every possible permutation of letter, but we will go through the more prevalent ones. The thought to hold on to is that typically (not always) a company who has their financial statements audited annually will tend to have better accounting systems and policies. In order for the accountants to issue unqualified opinions on their audits, the policies, procedures, internal controls, and accuracy have to be there. Companies with adequate accounting policies, procedures, internal controls, and accuracy generate timely and accurate financial information. Timely and accurate financial information leads to good financial decisions. Good financial decisions lead to financial success. In addition, the companies that get unqualified opinions on their financial statements tend to be more ethical.

A typical Independent Auditors' Report will be titled as such. It will be addressed to the Board of Directors/Stockholders of the company. The report will have three paragraphs. Those paragraphs are known as the introductory paragraph, the scope paragraph, and the opinion paragraph. These paragraphs will appear in that order. The report will be signed and dated by the firm who performed the audit. The introductory paragraph will include the following: a statement that the financial statements were audited, name of the entity being audited, type of legal entity (i.e., corporation, partnership, limited liability Company, or sole proprietorship), date of the financial statements, identification of the financial statements (i.e., balance sheet, statement of income, retained earnings, and cash flows), statement of management responsibility, and statement of auditor responsibility.

The scope paragraph will discuss how Generally Accepted Auditing Standards (GAAS) was used, a statement about reasonable assurance, description of the audit process, and a reasonable basis for opinion. The opinion paragraph will delineate the identification of the financial statements, whether they present fairly in all material respects, financial position (balance sheet), results of operations (statement of income), cash flows, company name, dates, and whether in conformity with Generally Accepted Accounting Principles (GAAP). Exhibit 8.2 is an example of an unqualified opinion expressed on Pontrelli Recycling, Inc. by Bean and Counter, P.C. certified public accountants (see online exhibits).

In Exhibit 8.3, there is a fourth paragraph added and an except for reference in the opinion letter. Unless you have had the proper training and a full understanding of the issue causing the Qualified Opinion, it will be difficult to determine the effect of the issue on your potential client's finances. You should inquire as to why the position that caused the Qualified Opinion was taken by management. It should

EXHIBIT 8.2 An Unqualified Opinion/Independent Auditors' Report

---

INDEPENDENT AUDITORS' REPORT

To the Board of Directors and Stockholders of Pontrelli Recycling, Inc.

We have audited the accompanying balance sheet of Pontrelli Recycling, Inc. (a New Jersey corporation) as of December 31, 2010, and the related statements of income, retained earnings, and cash flows for the year then ended. These financial statements are the responsibility of the Company's management. Our responsibility is to express an opinion on these financial statements based on our audit.

We conducted our audit in accordance with auditing standards generally accepted in the United States of America. Those standards require that we plan and perform the audit to obtain reasonable assurance about whether the financial statements are free of material misstatement. An audit includes examining, on a test basis, evidence supporting the amounts and disclosures in the financial statements. An audit also includes assessing the accounting principles used and significant estimates made by management, as well as evaluating the overall financial statement presentation. We believe that our audit provides a reasonable basis for our opinion.

In our opinion, the financial statements referred to above present fairly, in all material respects, the financial position of Pontrelli Recycling, Inc. as of December 31, 2010, and the results of its operations and its cash flows for the year then ended in conformity with accounting principles generally accepted in the United States of America.

Bean and Counter, P.C.
Newark, NJ
March 15, 2011

---

be abundantly clear that your potential client has demonstrated that they are capable of ignoring the advice of their professionals in a very public way and with consequences. That prospective client may have good reason to, but be guided accordingly.

EXHIBIT 8.3 Qualified Opinion/Independent Auditors' Report

INDEPENDENT AUDITORS' REPORT

To the Board of Directors and Stockholders of Pontrelli Recycling, Inc.

We have audited the accompanying balance sheet of Pontrelli Recycling, Inc. (a New Jersey corporation) as of December 31, 2010, and the related statements of income, retained earnings, and cash flows for the year then ended. These financial statements are the responsibility of the Company's management. Our responsibility is to express an opinion on these financial statements based on our audit.

We conducted our audit in accordance with auditing standards generally accepted in the United States of America. Those standards require that we plan and perform the audit to obtain reasonable assurance about whether the financial statements are free of material misstatement. An audit includes examining, on a test basis, evidence supporting the amounts and disclosures in the financial statements. An audit also includes assessing the accounting principles used and significant estimates made by management, as well as evaluating the overall financial statement presentation. We believe that our audit provides a reasonable basis for our opinion.

The Company's financial statements do not disclose the amount of future commitments under long-term leases. In our opinion, disclosure of that information is required to conform to accounting principles generally accepted in the United States of America; however, management believes it is impracticable to develop the information.

In our opinion, except for the omission of the information discussed in the preceding paragraph, the financial statements referred to above present fairly, in all material respects, the financial position of Pontrelli Recycling, Inc. as of December 31, 2010, and the results of its operations and its cash flows for the year then ended in conformity with accounting principles generally accepted in the United States of America.

Bean and Counter, P.C.
Newark, NJ
March 15, 2011

Exhibit 8.4 is an example of a Disclaimer of Opinion. If your prospective client receives a letter like the one in Exhibit 8.5, then there had to be a pervasive scope limitation placed upon the auditors'

EXHIBIT 8.4 Adverse Opinion—Independent Auditors' Report

INDEPENDENT AUDITORS' REPORT

To the Board of Directors and Stockholders of Pontrelli Recycling, Inc.

We have audited the accompanying balance sheet of Pontrelli Recycling, Inc. (a New Jersey corporation) as of December 31, 2010, and the related statements of income, retained earnings, and cash flows for the year then ended. These financial statements are the responsibility of the Company's management. Our responsibility is to express an opinion on these financial statements based on our audit.

We conducted our audit in accordance with auditing standards generally accepted in the United States of America. Those standards require that we plan and perform the audit to obtain reasonable assurance about whether the financial statements are free of material misstatement. An audit includes examining, on a test basis, evidence supporting the amounts and disclosures in the financial statements. An audit also includes assessing the accounting principles used and significant estimates made by management, as well as evaluating the overall financial statement presentation. We believe that our audit provides a reasonable basis for our opinion.

As discussed in Note 24 to the financial statements, on April 24, 2010, judgment was entered against the Company in a lawsuit resulting in a liability to the Company of $1,000,000. The liability has been excluded from the accompanying balance sheet. In our opinion, the liability should be recorded to conform with accounting principles generally accepted in the United States of America. If the liability were recorded, accounts payable would be increased by $1,000,000, and retained earnings would be decreased by $600,000 as of December 31, 2010, and net income would be decreased by $600,000 for the year then ended.

(continued)

EXHIBIT 8.4 (*Continued*)

In our opinion, because of the effects of the matter discussed in the preceding paragraph, the financial statements referred to above do not present fairly, in conformity with accounting principles generally accepted in the United States of America, the financial position of Pontrelli Recycling, Inc. as of December 31, 2010, or the results of its operations or its cash flows for the year then ended.

Bean and Counter, P.C.
Newark, NJ
March 15, 2011

EXHIBIT 8.5 Disclaimer of Opinion—Independent Auditors' Report

INDEPENDENT AUDITORS' REPORT

To the Board of Directors and Stockholders of Pontrelli Recycling, Inc.

We were engaged to audit the accompanying balance sheet of Pontrelli Recycling, Inc. (a New Jersey corporation) as of December 31, 2010, and the related statements of income, retained earnings, and cash flows for the year then ended. These financial statements are the responsibility of the Company's management.

Detailed property, plant, and equipment records have not been maintained and certain prior-year records and supporting data were not available for our audit. Therefore, we were not able to satisfy ourselves about the amounts at which property, plant, and equipment, and related accumulated depreciation are recorded in the accompany balance sheet at December 31, 2010 (stated at $814,119 and $600,000, respectively), and the amount of depreciation expense for the year then ended (stated at $154,997).

Because of the significance of the matters discussed in the preceding paragraph, the scope of our work was not sufficient to enable us to express, and we do not express, an opinion on the financial statements referred to in the first paragraph.

Bean and Counter, P.C.
Newark, NJ
March 15, 2011

procedures. In other words, your potential client would not allow the auditors to do what they needed to or they refused to supply prerequisite documentation. Exhibit 8.5 specifically relates to inadequate accounting records. If your client is not willing to provide minimum documentation to their auditors or allow them to do their job, then you have to consider what they will do to you during your engagement.

In addition to the type of financial reports, your potential client may have other types of audits performed. These other types of audits include, but are not limited to, director exams, internal control audits, special agreed upon procedures audits, and other external audits on compliance issues. These additional audits are costly to the organization. The important thing to note beyond the presence of these audits is how the organization reacts to the findings. How proactive the organization is usually indicates its commitment to excellence.

An Unqualified Opinion with required explanatory language is issued when there's a concern by the auditor that the company being audited is not going to continue as a going concern in the ensuing 12 months. The following is a non-inclusive list of some of the conditions and events that may cause the auditor to question whether or not your prospective client will be a going concern:

- Recurring operating losses
- Working capital shortages
- Negative cash flow from operations
- Adverse key financial ratios
- Default on loan or similar agreements
- Dividend arrearages
- Denial or contraction of usual trade credit from suppliers
- Restructuring of debt
- Market conditions
- Key man turnover
- Inadequately equipped to enter into new markets
- Need for new sources of financing
- Need to liquidate substantial assets

- Technical default or breach of financial covenants
- Labor issues
- Unprofitable long-term commitments
- Substantial dependence on the success of a particular project
- Need to significantly revise operations
- Litigation and legal proceedings
- Legislation or other statutory matters that might jeopardize the company's ability to operate
- Loss of intellectual property
- Loss of critical customer or vendor
- Under- or uninsured casualty losses

The problem with having a potential client with one of these auditors' opinions is not with the integrity of the client, but with your ability to complete the project and get paid. At the risk of stating the obvious you need to be paid up front. However, there are certain laws in regard to preferential payments to creditors that may cause you to refund your payment in federal and state courts despite having provided the service. Please consult an attorney familiar with the bankruptcy rules in your jurisdiction about such matters before committing to the engagement. Exhibit 8.6 is an example of an Unqualified Opinion with required explanatory language specifically dealing with going concern.

EXHIBIT 8.6 Unqualified Opinion with Required Explanatory Language/ Independent Auditors' Report

---

INDEPENDENT AUDITORS' REPORT

To the Board of Directors and Stockholders of Pontrelli Recycling, Inc.

We have audited the accompanying balance sheet of Pontrelli Recycling, Inc. (a New Jersey corporation) as of December 31, 2010, and the related statements of income, retained earnings, and cash flows for the year ended. These financial statements are the responsibility of the Company's

EXHIBIT 8.6 (*Continued*)

management. Our responsibility is to express an opinion on these financial statements based on our audit.

We conducted our audit in accordance with auditing standards generally accepted in the United States of America. Those standards require that we plan and perform the audit to obtain reasonable assurance about whether the financial statements are free of material misstatement. An audit includes examining, on a test basis, evidence supporting the amounts and disclosures in the financial statements. An audit also includes assessing the accounting principles used and significant estimates made by management, as well as evaluating the overall financial statement presentation. We believe that our audit provides a reasonable basis for our opinion.

In our opinion, the financial statements referred to above present fairly, in all material respects, the financial position of Pontrelli Recycling, Inc. as of December 31, 2010, and the results of its operations and its cash flows for the year then ended in conformity with accounting principles generally accepted in the United States of America.

The accompanying financial statements have been prepared assuming that the Company will continue as a going concern. As discussed in Note 25 to the financial statements, the Company has been ordered by the State of New Jersey to cease operations as a recycling yard at its present location and has revoked its operating permits, which raise substantial doubt about its ability to continue as a going concern. Management's plans regarding those matters are described in Note 25. The financial statements do not include any adjustments that might result from the outcome of this uncertainty.

Bean and Counter, P.C.
Newark, NJ
March 15, 2011

The next class of letters is called the Independent Accountants' Review Report. As indicated earlier, the auditors refer to the body of work required to issue this type of report as a review of their client's financial statements. The review procedures are substantially less in scope than what is required for an audit. We cannot emphasize enough that the investigations and procedures for a review are substantially less than that of an audit. It is important to note that a review report is substantially better than an Adverse Opinion, Disclaimer of Opinion, or an Unqualified Opinion with required explanatory language. The only question is—had the auditor performed an audit instead of a review, would they have discovered information that would have caused them to issue an Adverse Opinion, Disclaimer of Opinion, or an Unqualified Opinion with required explanatory language? Exhibit 8.7 is an example of an Independent Accountants' Review Report.

EXHIBIT 8.7 Independent Accountants' Review Report

INDEPENDENT ACCOUNTANTS' REVIEW REPORT

To the Board of Directors and Stockholders of Pontrelli Recycling, Inc.

We have reviewed the accompanying balance sheet of Pontrelli Recycling, Inc. (a corporation) as of December 31, 2010, and the related statements of income and retained earnings and cash flows for the year then ended. A review includes primarily applying analytical procedures to management's (the owners') financial data and making inquiries of Company management (the owners). A review is substantially less in scope than an audit, the objective of which is the expression of an opinion regarding the financial statements as a whole. Accordingly, we do not express such an opinion.

Management is (The owners are) responsible for the preparation and fair representation of the financial statements in accordance with accounting principles generally accepted in the United States of America and for designing, implementing, and maintaining internal control relevant to the preparation and fair presentation of the financial statements.

Our responsibility is to conduct the review in accordance with Statements on Standards for Accounting and Review Services issued by the American Institute of Certified Public Accountants. Those standards require us to perform procedures to obtain limited assurance that there are no material modifications that should be made to the financial statements. We believe that the results of our procedures provide a reasonable basis for our report.

EXHIBIT 8.7 (*Continued*)

Based on our review, we are not aware of any material modifications that should be made to the accompanying financial statements in order for them to be in conformity with accounting principles generally accepted in the United States of America.

> Bean and Counter, P.C.
> Newark, NJ
> March 15, 2011

Unlike the audit reports, you really only have to be aware of one other variation of the review report. Exhibit 8.8 is an example of a review report when the client deviates from GAAP. Be mindful of those potential clients who don't follow rules and regulations.

EXHIBIT 8.8 Independent Accountants' Review Report with a Departure from GAAP

INDEPENDENT ACCOUNTANTS' REVIEW REPORT

To the Board of Directors and Stockholders of Pontrelli Recycling, Inc.

We have reviewed the accompanying balance sheet of Pontrelli Recycling, Inc. (a corporation) as of December 31, 2010, and the related statements of income and retained earnings and cash flows for the year then ended. A review includes primarily applying analytical procedures to management's (the owners') financial data and making inquiries of Company management (the owners). A review is substantially less in scope than an audit, the objective of which is the expression of an opinion regarding the financial statements as a whole. Accordingly, we do not express such an opinion.

Management is (The owners are) responsible for the preparation and fair representation of the financial statements in accordance with accounting principles generally accepted in the United States of America and for designing, implementing, and maintaining internal control relevant to the preparation and fair presentation of the financial statements.

(*continued*)

EXHIBIT 8.8 (*Continued*)

Our responsibility is to conduct the review in accordance with Statements on Standards for Accounting and Review Services issued by the American Institute of Certified Public Accountants. Those standards require us to perform procedures to obtain limited assurance that there are no material modifications that should be made to the financial statements. We believe that the results of our procedures provide a reasonable basis for our report.

Based on our review, with the exception of the matter described in the following paragraph, we are not aware of any material modifications that should be made to the accompanying financial statements in order for them to be in conformity with accounting principles generally accepted in the United States of America.

The Company's financial statements do not disclose that, during 2010, the Company purchased significant amounts of scrap aluminum at discounted prices from Barry Van Dyke, Inc., which is owned by certain directors of Pontrelli Recycling, Inc. It is possible that the terms of such purchases are not the same as those that would result from transactions among unrelated parties. These purchases accounted for 28% of the scrap aluminum purchased during 2010. Disclosure of that information is required by accounting principles generally accepted in the United States of America.

Bean and Counter, P.C.
Newark, NJ
March 15, 2011

The third and final class of letter that you will find with a potential client's financial statements are the Accountants' Compilation Report. At the risk of oversimplification, an accountant essentially reads the financial statements for format, reasonableness, and math accuracy. Accountants refer to the body of work required as a compilation. As you can imagine, you shouldn't rely on these types of financials. There are four variations of this report that you should be aware of. Exhibit 8.9 is an example of a typical Accountants' Compilation Report.

EXHIBIT 8.9 Independent Accountants' Compilation Report

INDEPENDENT ACCOUNTANTS' COMPILATION REPORT

To the Board of Directors and Stockholders of Pontrelli Recycling, Inc.

We have compiled the accompanying balance sheet of Pontrelli Recycling, Inc. (a corporation) as of December 31, 2010, and the related statements of income and retained earnings and cash flows for the year then ended. We have not audited or reviewed the accompanying financial statements and, accordingly, do not express an opinion or provide any assurance about whether the financial statements are in accordance with accounting principles generally accepted in the United States of America.

Management is (The owners are) responsible for the preparation and fair presentation of the financial statements in accordance with accounting principles generally accepted in the United States of America and for designing, implementing, and maintaining internal control relevant to the preparation and fair presentation of the financial statements.

Our responsibility is to conduct the compilation in accordance with Statements on Standards for Accounting and Review Services issued by the American Institute of Certified Public Accountants. The objective of a compilation is to assist management (the owners) in presenting financial information in the form of financial statements without undertaking to obtain or provide any assurance that there are no material modifications that should be made to the financial statements.

> Bean and Counter, P.C.
> Newark, NJ
> March 15, 2011

Exhibit 8.10 is an example of a Compilation report where the accountants are not independent. This type of letter is needed when it would appear that the accountant's judgment could be impaired. Some examples of this include, but are not limited to, the accountant or someone in the accounting firm having a financial interest in the entity, blood or marriage relationship to the owners or management, and monies owed between the parties. It is important to note that if

EXHIBIT 8.10 Accountants' Compilation Report/Lack of Independence

ACCOUNTANTS' COMPILATION REPORT

To the Board of Directors and Stockholders of Pontrelli Recycling, Inc.

We have compiled the accompanying balance sheet of Pontrelli Recycling. Inc. (a corporation) as of December 31, 2010, and the related statements of income and retained earnings and cash flows for the year then ended. We have not audited or reviewed the accompanying financial statements and, accordingly, do not express an opinion or provide any assurance about whether the financial statements are in accordance with accounting principles generally accepted in the United States of America.

Management is (The owners are) responsible for the preparation and fair presentation of the financial statements in accordance with accounting principles generally accepted in the United States of America and for designing, implementing, and maintaining internal control relevant to the preparation and fair presentation of the financial statements.

Our responsibility is to conduct the compilation in accordance with Statements on Standards for Accounting and Review Services issued by the American Institute of Certified Public Accountants. The objective of a compilation is to assist management (the owners) in presenting financial information in the form of financial statements without undertaking to obtain or provide any assurance that there are no material modifications that should be made to the financial statements.

We are not independent with respect to Pontrelli Recycling, Inc.

Bean and Counter, P.C.
Newark, NJ
March 15, 2011

there is an independence issue between the accounting firm and the client, then the accounting firm is prohibited from performing an audit or review.

Exhibit 8.11 is an example of the letter that is issued when a compilation is performed but all of the notes to the financial statements are omitted. This version of financial statements is the bare bones

EXHIBIT 8.11 Independent Accountants' Compilation Report/Substantially All Disclosures Omitted

INDEPENDENT ACCOUNTANTS' COMPILATION REPORT

To the Board of Directors and Stockholders of Pontrelli Recycling, Inc.

We have compiled the accompanying balance sheet of Pontrelli Recycling, Inc. (a corporation) as of December 31, 2010, and the related statements of income and retained earnings and cash flows for the year then ended. We have not audited or reviewed the accompanying financial statements and, accordingly, do not express an opinion or provide any assurance about whether the financial statements are in accordance with accounting principles generally accepted in the United States of America.

Management is (The owners are) responsible for the preparation and fair presentation of the financial statements in accordance with accounting principles generally accepted in the United States of America and for designing, implementing, and maintaining internal control relevant to the preparation and fair presentation of the financial statements.

Our responsibility is to conduct the compilation in accordance with Statements on Standards for Accounting and Review Services issued by the American Institute of Certified Public Accountants. The objective of a compilation is to assist management (the owners) in presenting financial information in the form of financial statements without undertaking to obtain or provide any assurance that there are no material modifications that should be made to the financial statements.

Management has (The owners have) elected to omit substantially all of the disclosures required by accounting principles generally accepted in the United States of America. If the omitted disclosures were included in the financial statements, they might influence the user's conclusions about the Company's financial position, results of operations, and cash flows. Accordingly, the financial statements are not designed for those who are not informed about such matters.

Bean and Counter, P.C.
Newark, NJ
March 15, 2011

version of presentation and procedures that is necessary in order to issue financial statements by an outside accountant.

Exhibit 8.12 is the fourth and final example of a Compilation report. This version is used when the company faces a major uncertainty. You need to be very careful when you run across one of these. Not unlike the going concern opinion for the audit, you need to be concerned as to whether the event described in the last paragraph will prove to be fatal to your potential client independent of their opinions.

EXHIBIT 8.12 Independent Accountants' Compilation Report/ Major Uncertainty

---

INDEPENDENT ACCOUNTANTS' COMPILATION REPORT

To the Board of Directors and Stockholders of Pontrelli Recycling, Inc.

We have compiled the accompanying balance sheet of Pontrelli Recycling, Inc. (a corporation) as of December 31, 2010, and the related statements of income and retained earnings and cash flows for the year then ended. We have not audited or reviewed the accompanying financial statements and, accordingly, do not express an opinion or provide any assurance about whether the financial statements are in accordance with accounting principles generally accepted in the United States of America.

Management is (The owners are) responsible for the preparation and fair presentation of the financial statements in accordance with accounting principles generally accepted in the United States of America and for designing, implementing, and maintaining internal control relevant to the preparation and fair presentation of the financial statements.

Our responsibility is to conduct the compilation in accordance with Statements on Standards for Accounting and Review Services issued by the American Institute of Certified Public Accountants. The objective of a compilation is to assist management (the owners) in presenting financial information in the form of financial statements without undertaking to obtain or provide any assurance that there are no material modifications that should be made to the financial statements.

EXHIBIT 8.12 (*Continued*)

    As discussed in Note 24, the Company is currently named in a legal action. The Company has determined that it is not possible to predict the eventual outcome of the legal action but has determined that the resolution of the action will not result in an adverse judgment that would materially affect the financial statements. Accordingly, the accompanying financial statements do not include any adjustments related to the legal action under Financial Accounting Standards Board FASB ASC 450 (formerly Statement of Financial Accounting Standards No. 5, Accounting for Contingencies).

Bean and Counter, P.C.
Newark, NJ
March 15, 2011

Project Specific Risk

Before you begin execution of a project, risk assessment is a requirement. A good starting place is to identify threats to the milestones of the project. It is impossible to anticipate everything that could go wrong, neither is it practical to spend 10 years working on a risk assessment for a 90-day project. The objective here is to create a consciousness of the potential risks that should be addressed in the planning of the project. Here is a list of questions to start with:

1. What is the bargaining power of your suppliers of products or services? Are they easily substituted for?
2. Is there a threat of a new entrant into your marketplace?
3. What is the bargaining power of your customers? Can they substitute easily for you?
4. How easily are your products or services substituted for?
5. What is the rivalry amongst competitors?
6. What is the impact of governmental intervention?
7. Are there regulatory compliance issues?
8. How will project failure damage the Company's reputation?
9. Is there on-going litigation?

10. Is the Company or project located in an area prone to natural disasters, including but not limited to flooding, tornados, earthquakes, fire, and environmental?
11. Does the Company or project rely on a key person?
12. Can the funding of the project become an issue?

The first five questions are attributed to Michael Porter and are known as Porter's Five Forces. In this context these questions are used to set up an external environmental understanding of the company's competitive forces. An understanding of these competitive forces will highlight your company's strengths, weaknesses, opportunities, and threats (SWOT).

Question number six is for the purpose of determining whether your company will be affected by political intervention, regulatory intervention, a change in income or excise tax policies, and tariffs. In regard to question number seven, you need to determine whether or not your company and your project are subject to any Federal, State, and/or local regulations. In addition, you need to determine whether they can be compliant and the associated cost of compliance. If your project needs to be compliant, then be mindful of the potential civil and criminal penalties for failing to be compliant.

Be especially mindful if you can be held accountable for compliance. If you can, then you should make arrangements for how your company is going to bear the cost to defend you from the government. Needless to say, you should make certain that you know what you are doing—that you will be in control of ensuring compliance.

Question eight is to understand how, if at all, a failed project will affect the rest of the organization (see the Creating a Project Budget section in Chapter 7). The idea here is to plan in such a way that a less-than-expected result causes the fewest negative consequences for the organization. An example here would be British Petroleum (BP) undertaking a project that could have catastrophic results on the environment after their 2010 debacle in the Gulf of Mexico.

In regard to question number nine, it is important to know whether or not your project could become mired in litigation. Important issues to consider here are: How much will the litigation cost? How will those costs be funded? Will the litigation take management away from their duties and focus? Finally, what are the consequences of an adverse ruling?

For question number 10, the focus is on whether or not your potential client is insured against these natural disasters. If they are not insured, then are they insurable? Is the cost to insure prohibitive? Besides the cost of a natural disaster, one has to consider the time delays on completing a project. In addition to the natural disasters, one has to consider the effects of terrorism on your potential client and your project.

Finally, in number 11, the purpose is to identify key employees and contingency plans for a substitute or replacement. In regard to question number 12, the objective is to gain an understanding of how secure the funding is for your project and the contingency plan for substitution funding. Borrowing arrangements and funding can change as a result of changes in economic conditions, changes in your potential client's financial performance, and changes to the finances of those supplying the funding.

Engagement Acceptance

Once you have completed the risk assessment, someone must decide whether or not to accept the project. The following questions will guide you to that decision:

- Do you have the competency and availability/manpower to perform the engagement to the level your client is expecting?
- Do you have any reasons to doubt your client's integrity or honesty?
- Is the organizational structure conducive to the way you like to work?

- Do they have the appropriate manpower for you to work with?
- Is there anything in their accountant's report on the financial statements that you should be concerned with?
- Is there anything in the project specific risk that makes the success of the project unlikely?
- Will the acceptance of this engagement cause a conflict of interest with other existing or potential clients?
- Are you concerned about being paid for your services?
- Will you make a profit on this engagement?

As indicated earlier, you will have to answer these questions honestly and the decision is left to you.

Conclusion

Many times when things go awry, we say "I had a feeling something was amiss". You may become overwhelmed with the planning of the engagement. The demands of initiating and planning the project can cause you to narrow your focus or become distracted, causing you to lose sight of the warning signs in the background. The objective of this chapter is to make you consciously acknowledge the potential pitfalls in your engagement. It is the intent of this chapter to supply a guideline for assessing the possibility of being unpleasantly surprised (risk) associated with accepting a given engagement.

It is easy to answer all of the questions posed in this chapter and walk away from a less-than-desirable engagement when you have more than enough work and money. We hope that all of you are in that situation. For those who are not and choose to take that less-than-desirable engagement, make note of the dangers and plan accordingly. Be prepared.

About the Web Site

The Exhibits from Chapter 8, Risk Assessment, can also be found on the Internet at www.wiley.com/go/pmaccounting. These exhibits are meant to illustrate the different types of findings that a Certified Public Accountant of an accounting firm may issue following an audit. They are for illustration purposes only.

Index